To William,

With best wishes,

Carole Hawkins

Ladymede leaver
2012

Never a Dull Moment

A biography of Peggy Batchelor
as told to Carole Hawkins

Carole Hawkins

authorHOUSE®

AuthorHouse™
1663 Liberty Drive
Bloomington, IN 47403
www.authorhouse.com
Phone: 1-800-839-8640

First published by AuthorHouse   01/03/2012

ISBN: 978-1-4678-8250-7 (sc)
ISBN: 978-1-4678-8249-1 (ebk)

Printed in the United States of America

Any people depicted in stock imagery provided by Thinkstock are models, and such images are being used for illustrative purposes only.
Certain stock imagery © Thinkstock.

This book is printed on acid-free paper.

INTRODUCTION

One balmy spring day in 2008, a group of U3A members gathered in a small hall in Tring. It was their regular monthly meeting and few members seemed to know who was coming to speak to them. They enjoyed a cup of tea and a chat and then sat down to listen to the "business" part of the meeting. It has to be said that the general attention span was not good.

Then a diminutive figure took the stage.

Peggy Batchelor's strong, melodious voice filled the room; the audience were spellbound. For 90 minutes she held their rapt attention as story after story of her extraordinary wartime experiences were unveiled.

At the end, they wanted more, much more; and then someone asked the question,

"Have you ever written a book?"

No, Peggy had not, and over lunch and several glasses of wine, we discussed the possibilities of recording this amazing life story for posterity.

This is Peggy's book

CONTENTS

CHAPTER 1

THE BEGINNING

The Early Years

There was nearly no story to tell.

Peggy was born in 1916 at her Aunt's nursing home and was pronounced stillborn. However, her Aunt would not give up on the tiny child and eventually coaxed Peggy to life, the first extraordinary moment in what was to be a highly eventful life.

She was, however, born with congenital spondylitis of the lumbar vertebrae which was painful but, a determined character right from the start, she never let it interfere with her life in any way.

Peggy grew up in a loving family and was blessed with musical parents.

Her Mother played the piano and her Father sang. From a very small baby, Peggy would be taken to musical evenings, put in a chair from which she watched and listened as the music was played. She could always be relied upon to sit absolutely still and be entirely focussed on the music and performance around her. Her love of words came from her Father, who had a wonderful collection of books, none of which were ever out of bounds to Peggy. At an early age she read avidly, even her Father's most valuable books.

Performance was a natural part of life for all the family. Peggy did not realise that her ability and various opportunities to perform were in any way special. She thought all children did this. Her first performances were with her parents who used to go around various villages helping to raise money for the churches. Mother played the piano, sang and did monologues and Father sang. As soon as she could toddle, Peggy too played her part. She even accompanied her parents to a leper hospital, The Home of St Giles at East Hanningfield in Essex—a useful experience for later life for when she visited West Africa, the lepers held no fears for her—, and she went to Rochford mental hospital, which was not a happy experience as she went into a padded cell which made her suffer from claustrophobia for years.

There were happy holidays which also had an element of early performance.

Peggy's Father knew someone who had a chauffeur driven Daimler who would fetch the Batchelor family and take them to a guest house for an annual holiday. Both the car and the holiday were not at all common in the immediate post Great War period, but tiny Peggy was unaware of this and loved the ride in the car and each evening her Father would lift her up and she stood on the grand piano of the holiday house and sang for the assembled adults. She particularly remembers singing "Away in a Manger" at the age of four, and singing "Alice Blue Gown", and being particularly fond of her very own little blue dress which was more of a forget-me-not blue.

Peggy's Mother sang in the semi professional Henry Jaxon choir which used to augment the chorus at Covent Garden, Sadler's Wells and the Albert Hall. Little Peggy watched all the great operas from the wings.

(Peggy's parents on their wedding day)

Wembley

Then her own first big moment came in 1925 at the big Wembley Tattoo which was part of the Empire Exhibition.

The Henry Jaxon choir were all dressed as Cockneys and the children were part of the group. Peggy's Mother was part of the choir. Peggy was resplendent in a little dress and a torn pinafore and a red hat. Just as they were leaving the house, her Mother added a Union Jack flag to the ensemble. This proved to be a key addition.

At Wembley the children were asked to walk in front of the band. Peggy watched the soldiers and as soon as the music started, she marched like they did. This proved to be a major hit with the crowd and gradually the other children were taken off. Peggy marched alone. This was fine until she realised what was happening and she tried to run back to the safety of her Mother's arms. However, she was persuaded to continue, and she danced and marched, changing her steps to match the music. When the Scottish regiments were marching and playing, she did a Highland Fling and then changed to a sailor's Hornpipe when the music changed. All of this was entirely impromptu and unrehearsed but the natural performer shone through and

Peggy was invited to take part in every performance. Her Mother was not entirely sure that this was a good thing and said she would have to consult her husband, but he was away on business, and in the era before most people had telephones, he could not be contacted. Mother, therefore, had to make the decision alone and fortunately for Peggy, she decided to say yes.

So Peggy became "Baby Peggy of the Wembley Tattoo", dancing across the huge new stadium on her own four times a performance. It was quickly realised that it was too much for her to run back across the stadium each time and so she was carried back by a large policeman.

Baby Peggy danced before the crowned heads of Europe and all the visiting dignitaries. She even had the permission of the King to have her photograph taken with the Guards.

Every day she would travel to Wembley with her Mother and then, after she had performed, she would travel back in a car, accompanied by a young lady called Nancy, whose Mother ran a fish and chip shop, a very exciting place in Peggy's eyes. Nancy would then look after her until her Mother, whose own performance commitment lasted way into the evening, arrived home.

At the end of the Tattoo, another honour awaited her. She was the guest of honour at a special tea given by the management of the Stadium Restaurant for the troops who had taken part in the Tattoo. This, for Peggy, was one of the most exciting things that had ever happened in her young life. She was too excited to eat and told one newspaper, *"I can eat cream cakes any day but I cannot see all my big soldier friends at a party like this, I have never been to such a party before—and I want it to go on for a long time."*

This zest for getting the maximum from any experience and to enjoy every moment was to last a lifetime and it captivated the nation.

Her love of people was also apparent. She told the Daily Express, *"I love them all."*

Peggy delighted the newspapers of the day. The "News" wrote an article called "At Home with Baby Peggy Batchelor" with the sub heading "Troubled about Teddy"

They wrote *"the most talked about person in the Searchlight and Torchlight Tattoo in the Stadium is an eight year old Wembley schoolgirl, Miss Peggy Joyce Batchelor . . . ."* I am very worried," she confided to the News representative *when he called on her. "I want to take my Teddy Bear to see the Tattoo but I don't know where I can put him when I am doing my part. I can't leave him all by himself or he will be lonely, and, well, what would you do?"*

The article goes on to say that Peggy was delighted that the Tattoo was to go on for another two weeks and thought that she might come up with a Teddy solution before then. She was a little worried that her Mother had said she could not go to Wembley if the weather turned cold, *"But,"* she told the journalist, *"I shall be able to bring her round all right." "And,"* continued the article *"Peggy smiled a big baby smile that would have melted the heart of anyone".*

Individuals wrote to the newspapers about Peggy and directly to her and one elderly gentleman presented her with a crown, which was a five shilling piece, an unusual coin by that time, because he was so impressed with her dancing. Another wrote to the Daily Graphic portraying Peggy as the spirit of the Tattoo saying, *"One tiny figure . . . . remains in memory. So light and childlike in her movements and yet riveting every eye of the vast audience . . . . What power is here . . . . it is true for us . . . and a little child shall lead them".*

(Peggy in her Wembley Tattoo costume)

Her official thanks came from the Lieutenant General in charge of the event. Clearly this man was used to dictating formal letters but his genuine pleasure at her contribution shines through the formal language as in his own hand he crossed through the salutation to "Miss Batchelor" replacing it with "Peggy".

FOREIGN OFFICE AND BOARD OF TRADE.

DEPARTMENT OF OVERSEAS TRADE

(DEVELOPMENT AND INTELLIGENCE),

35, OLD QUEEN STREET,

2nd November, 1925. S.W.1.

TELEPHONE
VICTORIA 9040.

Peggy

Dear ~~Miss Batchelor~~,

The Exhibition is over. The Torchlight and
Searchlight Tattoo is a memory. My Committee and I
wish to lose no time in sending you individually our
very sincere thanks for the time and trouble you have
so generously given during so many weeks since last May
to help us in the production of "London Defended"
and now during the long ten weeks' run of the Tattoo.

It must at any rate be a satisfaction to you,
as it is to us, that the Tattoo should have met with
such an unparalleled success. The introduction in
which you and the other members of Mr. Jaxon's choir
played so conspicuous a part as well as your unaccom-
panied singing of the Evening Hymn in the finale were
both outstanding features in the programme and will
be happy memories to nearly two millions of your
fellow citizens for many years to come.

I am to ask you to accept from us a small
memento of the Tattoo which will be sent to you early
next month. It has been specially designed for this
purpose and has been made for you by the Ashtead
Potters, who are all badly disabled men who received
their injuries in the Great War.

Believe me,
Yours sincerely and gratefully,

[signature]

Lieutenant General,
Government Stadium Displays Committee.

Miss P.Batchelor,
29, Clayton Avenue,
Wembley, Middx.

(The letter of thanks)

11

"Her" policeman also presented her with a hand written scroll tied with a red ribbon as a memento of the occasion which she has always kept.

(Scroll from her Policeman)

Peggy was then asked to dance at other events, all of which seemed perfectly normal and natural to her. She still had no concept of being different from other children. She featured in the Ramblers Concert Party in aid of the Hanwell Boy Scouts in 1926 billed as "the drum major of the recent Wembley Tattoo".

And then came the film offer.

"Baby Peggy" was obviously very marketable. However, wisely Peggy's parents were extremely wary. In those days there were no chaperons in the film business, which itself was still relatively new and thus viewed with some suspicion. They decided that the offer should be rejected and so Peggy went from fame to oblivion, but still with very little concept of either.

Life continued as normal.

Growing Up

Growing up in 1920s Britain had a certain pattern to it. In common with most people, the weekly food was predictable, with a lovely roast beef lunch on Sundays, cold on Mondays, the leftovers being turned into a pie or a casserole on Tuesday, and there was always fish on Fridays. Fruit and vegetables were seasonal and milk was delivered daily by a milkman with a horse drawn cart. He would fill the metal can Peggy's Mother hung out on a hook over the back gate, and in summer, it had to be brought in quickly before the milk curdled. A French onion seller would come round periodically on a bicycle festooned with strings of tasty onions. The streets were very clean as the road sweeper came on his rounds daily. The street lights were gas and the lamplighter would come daily to light them and then to turn them off in the morning. Post was delivered three times a day and the postage rate was ½ d for a postcard and 1d for a letter.

The domestic routine was always the same too. In common with all her contemporaries, Peggy's Mother would do the washing on Mondays, the one day they had a cold main meal. She would use the household implement which all children found fascinating—the mangle, and Peggy would help to turn the handle. Ironing would be done on Tuesday, and great pride was taken in clean linen and neat ironing.

Friday night was always bath night and Peggy remembers the warm bath in front of the stove which was lovely. Other evenings, her Mother gave her a "wash down" in the bathroom which was a quick affair in the cold of the unheated bathroom in winter!

Wirelesses were the "must have" of the day and Peggy remembers one of her uncles making a crystal set in a cigar box and everyone trying to hear the broadcast clustered around two ear pieces, and one year to her great delight, "Uncle Mac" played a birthday request for her on Children's Hour. Birthdays were always exciting and she remembers hunting for her presents which had been hidden under the cushions of the settee!

Travel by train was always exciting, and the trains were of course steam trains which seemed almost to be living characters. Peggy's Father taught her the polite convention of the day that one always thanked the driver at the end of the journey. Even in these days of electric and diesel trains, this is a practice Peggy still follows.

Peggy started school at a little village school but it was not a success. Peggy was left handed but was made to use her right hand as was the practice in those days. Although it was initially difficult, she found in time she was ambidextrous, which was a great advantage in later life. She was then sent to Haberdashers' Aske's School, then in Creffield Road in West Acton. She travelled alone from the family home in

Alperton by train and her Mother arranged for the ticket collector at Ealing Common Station to see the diminutive 8 year old across the busy main road.

Peggy loved Haberdashers', ruled over by the formidable but kind Miss Sprules, but even then her school days were not without problems. She got into trouble for dancing on the platform at Ealing Common Station, this after having been recognised as "Baby Peggy". She was also spotted going into a fish and chip shop, not a venue regarded by Miss Sprules as suitable for a young Haberdasher! Peggy was in fact taking a message from her Mother to Nancy.

Peggy had been a little astonished when she had lunch on her first day at Haberdashers' and found that, horror of horrors, there were no tablecloths on the wooden tables and all the children had to sit on long wooden benches with a Prefect at the head of each table. This was a far cry from the pristine white tablecloths her Mother provided at home. The staff at the high table had white starched napkins however, so she was reassured by this. Another abiding memory from these early days at school was the Dorcas Society. The girls were required to knit woollen squares which were then made into blankets and sent to the Dorcas charity for distribution. Peggy remembers that her squares were never really square as she and the wool battled for supremacy. She was intrigued to find that the author had exactly the same experiences at the school in the late 1960s!

Peggy's happy school days at Acton were cut short by diphtheria. She lost a great deal of schooling and her parents were advised that their fragile daughter stood more chance of survival by the sea, and so the family moved to Leigh-on-Sea in Essex.

Peggy's Mother was determined that her daughter would not develop the local accent and so elocution lessons were arranged. Peggy loved these and entered festivals, took speech and drama examinations and joined dramatic societies. The foundations of her future career were built here.

Peggy was sent to Southend High School for Girls. She had been sent with a glowing reference from Miss Sprules, but no allowance was made for the fact that Peggy had missed most of a year's schooling and was therefore not up to the same standard as her contemporaries. Life at school was, unsurprisingly in these circumstances, not a success academically, and Peggy was always in trouble. Here her headmistress, Miss Swann, called her "a bitter disappointment". Peggy determined to live up to this accolade and thus saw a great deal of Miss Swann!!

However, she loved English and music; she led the second violins in the school orchestra, sang in the school choir, took part in every drama activity possible, and enjoyed sports, but, with her problems understanding numbers, she could not cope with the studying necessary for Matriculation, which loomed on the horizon. Peggy always did her homework diligently but suffered from what is now known as dyscalculia; numbers were largely a mystery to her. Wisely, her parents came to the rescue and paid for Peggy to leave school early and go for private music and drama lessons in London where she was inspired at Guildhall by her weekly lessons with Frank Ridley. She found she could learn scripts easily—a skill that would pay dividends in years to come in rep—and she practised every day at home. Aware that her parents were making sacrifices to allow her to have this unusual education, Peggy worked as an accompanist for the local dance school to pay for the 2/6 return fare to London twice weekly.

Peggy did not lack for company in these formative years. Her parents always had many visitors to the house and were tolerant, unusually for the time, of a wide variety of lifestyles. So Peggy came into contact with many problems such as teenagers who were pregnant, gay people who were victimised, and alcoholism, but she learnt that all lifestyles were acceptable and she gained much tolerance and wisdom from her parents. There was, for example, always alcohol in the house for visitors, but neither of her parents drank it. Her grandfather and aunt had been alcoholics. Grandfather had been a master builder and even had his own coach. His coachman would regularly have to bring him home in a drunken state and when he died the family found they were destitute. Peggy's Mother had to leave school and go to work as a nanny for her eldest brother's family. No wonder she shunned alcohol, but it is a measure of this remarkable woman that she did not judge badly others who drank it.

Peggy's Mother had been a psychiatric nurse and had therefore much insight into the problems people faced. She also very much believed that people should face up to their problems and overcome them. She was kind and loving to Peggy and would nurse her tenderly if she was really ill, but small ailments were dismissed, and Peggy was brought up not to cry over trivia. She also was brought up to tough things out. As a small child she witnessed a terrible accident whilst out with her aunt. Although her aunt tried to shield her from the sight, she saw and was horrified by a very gory scene, which left her with a fear of blood. Later as war began, she determined to put this behind her and did her St John's Ambulance training, facing the problem as she had been taught.

Peggy remembers a very happy childhood, but there was sadness too. Her Mother was frequently ill; she had further unsuccessful pregnancies and even a baby son, Robert who died in infancy. Indeed Peggy's earliest memory is standing in her cot and seeing her baby brother newly born. She is not sure whether she remembers or just had been told that she, her Mother and brother sheltered under the table during a Zeppelin raid.

As a child Peggy was aware of the sadness in the household when her brother died and as an only child she felt a sense of responsibility towards her parents as well as a deep love. She remembers aged about five or six helping her Mother tidy her Father's cupboard. In a drawer were a number of sports cups and awards her Father had won in his youth. Her Mother, unaware of the impact her words would have, told Peggy that Daddy had kept all of these things hoping that one day he would have a little boy to whom he could pass them. Peggy thought that this meant that her Father did not want her, but that he wanted a boy. Clearly he did not have the longed for son and so she determined that she would be that boy and do all of the sports that she could to please her Father. She, therefore, played all the school games such as netball and lacrosse and she played tennis, although she struggled with backhand due to a weak wrist. Whenever she could she would play cricket with the boys and because her Father played, she took up golf which she hated. For once the performer in her did not come out, and she preferred to tee off without an audience, tending to mishit horribly if anyone was watching, as she was aware of her deficiencies in the sport, and became more nervous if she was under scrutiny!

The only sport she really enjoyed was horse riding. She loved the animals and had the natural co-ordination to do well. Money was short and so her Father taught her the basics at home using two chairs and a piece of rope. Her parents kitted her out in a very smart riding outfit and she went to the riding school for the first time. Ever the actress, she copied the others and put into practice the skills learnt in the dining room. It was only after she had been out on her first hack that the owner of the stables found out she was a complete novice. He was furious, as she should have been on a leading rein, but because she had acquitted herself so well, he allowed her to continue and she loved every moment, knowing she was making her Father very proud. It was only many years later that she realised her Father loved her for herself and that he never regarded her as a poor substitute for a boy.

When her Mother was ill Peggy was sent to stay with her aunt and her cousin Harry who was very talented.

Peggy adored Harry and followed him everywhere and he, although in his teens, was remarkably loving and tolerant of his little cousin. Harry and his friends had a shed on a private beach where they used to meet. Peggy tagged along and remembers the boys put her up on a shelf where she sat and watched them play the most wonderful music. Harry played the violin but also could sing and dance. He was destined for a career on the stage and promised Peggy, "When I make it, Pegs, you are coming with me".

Harry took her out in his sailing yacht, nearly losing her when he capsized it. A typical teenager, he rescued the boat before the small girl! They went home soaked and shivering and Peggy remembers both she and Harry being stripped of their wet clothes in front of the fire and wrapped in big towels to warm up.

Peggy loved being with him but she did miss her Mother. Her aunt, mindful of her Mother's ill health and trying to alleviate the inevitable worry for her only child, always tried to assure her Mother that Peggy did not miss her, but when she was taken to the hospital to visit her, the little girl ran down the length of the ward, flung herself into her Mother's arms and hugged her fiercely, which was probably reassuring, if painful, for her Mother.

Harry became a professional entertainer and was due to play the lead in a West End Musical. Before he started, he had a little time to spare and so took a job leading an orchestra on a cruise ship. During their free time, crew members were allowed to go to the back of the ship's deck to an area out of bounds for the passengers. Harry, during one break, took his book and went out there. What happened next was never known but Harry disappeared. His absence was not noticed until he was due to perform again by which time it was too late. His body was never recovered and Peggy mourns him to this day.

All of these childhood experiences were to have a profound effect on her perception of adult life.

(Harry)

CHAPTER 2

EARLY CAREER

The Beginnings

Mindful that her parents were making significant sacrifices to support her career, Peggy worked very hard in the early 1930s to appear in as many productions as she could. She was part of the Southend-on-Sea Repertory Company, but she also appeared in various charity productions and was always learning a new part. In rep you always had three plays on the go, the one you were doing, the one you were rehearsing and the next one you were learning. Peggy's phenomenal memory helped here and she also retained previous parts in her memory to be revived if necessary. She performed in a wide range of genres too, everything from Mole in "Toad of Toad Hall" to Celia in "As you Like It".

In 1938 she appeared at the Royal Albert Hall in the presence of the Duchess of Gloucester in a special show to celebrate the Girls' Life Brigade. Peggy played a young Elizabeth I. In those days royalty were always portrayed on stage as dignified and aloof, especially in shows performed in front of current royalty. Peggy shocked her audience by running down the stairs on to the stage and playing the young Queen as an excited and vibrant young girl. After the initial shock had worn off, this portrayal was well received as most people appreciated that Peggy's version was nearer to reality than the expected staid rather wooden version.

From Fame to Oblivion

In January 1939, The Sunday Express ran an article called "From Fame to Oblivion". One of the people it featured on 16th January was "Baby Peggy" with the implication that after a brief moment of fame, she would never be heard of again.

They wrote, *"Two million people who saw the Wembley Tattoo of 1925 talked for weeks about the little girl in coster dress who danced every night before the massed bands and 2000 troops as she led them into the arena . . . . But after ten weeks of glory Peggy faded from public notice. Last week the Sunday Express discovered her again."*

Peggy told the paper that the experience had changed her mind from her childhood ambition to become a nurse to the ambition to pursue a career in the theatre and that at 21 that was exactly what she was doing. They managed to write this part of the report in a fairly dismissive manner.

Little did they know that Peggy's extraordinary story was just beginning.

CHAPTER 3

AND SO TO WAR

The Early Days

At the beginning of the war, now living in Devon where her Father would ultimately become a clergyman, Peggy was playing teenagers and young women for a local dramatic society. Influenced by her Father and his experiences of the Great War, Peggy was a member of the Peace Pledge Union and a dedicated pacifist. She took part in pacifist plays and used to go to pacifist meetings where George Lansbury would sign autographs using Peggy's back as a convenient writing desk. She was so anti war that she would not even collect her gas mask which was actually a criminal offence.

After Dunkirk, Peggy's Father asked her to go with him to Exeter station with a canteen to meet a troop train returning from the beaches. What she saw there shook Peggy to the core, and caused a complete change of attitude. She went home, immediately got a gas mask and joined the ARP. She drove a van during the air raids in Exmouth which became a mortuary van. Peggy stoically did her duty and refused to cry even when she had to recover the bodies of dead children. She saved her tears to shed in private. In the daytime in Exeter, she did salvage work—having lied about her ability to do shorthand to get the job, a job which actually never once required that skill. She salvaged the small items from bombed buildings such as jewellery which could be later claimed by their owners.

At this time her oratory skills were recognised and so she was sent to talk to various groups of people such as the dustmen about salvage, farmers, the W.I. and so on about collecting scrap metal for the war effort. All this was really using her skill as a performer and gained her many new and unlikely friends. It was not until many years later that she discovered that you could not actually make Spitfires out of old saucepans, but at the time she was convinced that she and her audiences were "doing their bit".

She was impassioned and convincing. During the Exmouth War Weapons Week, she appealed to her audiences to lend money. *"Isn't it worth a sacrifice to ensure they (the children) will never again experience the tragic times through which we are now passing?"*

She convinced them and the fund grew.

Peggy's knowledge of unusual subjects increased as the war progressed. One of the lectures she gave was on the subject of "Pig Swill", which she delivered with passion and enthusiasm to a gathering of farmers at Exeter market. So impressed were they that she received cheery waves and greetings from many of her audiences as she walked through the local towns. "Her" farmers and dustmen greeted her as long lost friends. Even in those difficult times Peggy proved how well she could connect with an audience.

Her real love of acting had been temporarily put on hold at the outbreak of war but as the numbers of men in uniform grew so did the need for quality entertainment

The Marines were encamped at Lympstone and the Buffs nearby, and Peggy and some of her contemporaries gave shows there. One of these shows led to an invitation to join ENSA—"Entertainments National Service Association", which was irreverently parodied as "Every Night Something Awful!" and so Peggy's war really began.

ENSA

The call to join ENSA was not so much an invitation as a call up. Peggy was ordered to report to the ENSA headquarters at the Theatre Royal Drury Lane where she faced a formidable audition panel, Basil Dean, who had founded ENSA, Henry Oscar, Lillian Braithwaite and Sybil Thorndike. The seats were covered in dust sheets and Peggy could not see her famous audience. This was something of a problem as she prepared to show them her "Snow White" which was based on audience participation and picking up cues from their responses. However, although she could not see them properly they joined in and were clearly impressed by the interactivity of the act. Sybil Thorndike asked what else she could offer and she did a Cockney number which again impressed them. The fact that she was such an accomplished pianist must have helped and Peggy was hired immediately.

Peggy's relationship with Sybil Thorndike was to be a life long one. Not only would Sybil ultimately become a patron of her school, but Peggy formed warm friendships with her sons, Christopher whom she visited on trips to Dublin, and John with whom she worked. Diana, Sybil's granddaughter would, many years later, perform a tribute to her famous grandmother with Peggy.

Sybil told her that they were starting hospital units straight away and she would work with these. Peggy phoned her parents to explain that she was staying in London and would find accommodation at the YWCA, and so began the career that would lead to high adventure, danger and the best and worst of times.

In 1941 Peggy joined ENSA initially with some appearances in concerts in London and then as part of scratch companies hastily put together to tour military hospitals and convalescent homes. She recalls going to entertain some of the wounded at Harewood House and was amazed to find fine furniture, wonderful pictures and valuable ornaments apparently randomly inter-dispersed between hospital beds and medical equipment. She asked the Countess why she had left all of her treasures out in this way. The Countess replied that the men were giving everything for us and so it was the least she could do. Peggy, an ardent socialist, was humbled by the reply and it made her review her opinion of the aristocracy.

There was a great element of secrecy about these missions and the performers would be sent instructions to go to a certain London station and be issued with a travel warrant but only the person in charge of the group, usually the star of the show, would know the actual destination.

On one such occasion, Peggy in a group under the eye of the established star, Violet Carson, travelled to East Grinstead. They were all blissfully unaware that East Grinstead was a cutting edge and somewhat experimental burns unit where soldiers, and particularly airmen, who had been badly burned in conflict and a few civilian casualties, received treatment from Archie McIndoe and his team. They pioneered new treatments and skin grafts and if they could not make the unfortunate victims beautiful, they at least could rebuild shattered faces and bodies and heal dreadful wounds to enable the injured to return to some semblance of normality. The inmates themselves were aware that they were "guinea pigs" and after the war the survivors formed the Guinea Pig Club.

The young ENSA troupe initially recoiled from the sights that faced them but Violet Carson was made of sterner stuff, having lived through the First World War. She insisted that they performed without flinching and that they brought laughter and enjoyment to lighten the mood of those who had suffered so much. When Peggy said she could not go back on stage, the formidable Violet, who was quite a large lady, took her by the shoulders, shook her none too gently and propelled her back towards the stage with the words, *"You are bloody well going on again"*.

Peggy felt after this experience that she could face anything.

CHAPTER 4

Service Abroad

West Africa

In the summer of 1942, Peggy was offered the opportunity to join an all girl concert party of five girls and go on tour overseas. The company was called "The Five Smart Girls" and they discovered that their destination was to be West Africa. This was a somewhat frightening prospect as Africa was still widely referred to as "The White Man's Grave", but given the air raids and the other dangers that Peggy had already faced and survived so far, she decided that this was not something to worry about too much.

It is interesting to note that the authorities expected the artistes to have very little knowledge of Africa. The kit list states that "*Artistes cannot possibly wear clothing as worn in England . . . It should also be noted that through heavy perspiration and constant washing clothes are useless after about three months, therefore expensive attire should be avoided. This applies to the 10 months HOT season".*

And so on 26th July 1942, Peggy met the others at Drury Lane at 10pm and together with another group they were to travel with, "The Music Box", they set off on a grand adventure, fortified by a box of food provided by Lyons. They travelled by troop train, much to the joy of the troops, who thought that the war was definitely taking a turn for the better when nine girls boarded their train. They joined their ship "Narkunda" the following afternoon and set sail on 30th July as part of a convoy. The danger of sea travel was all too evident and Peggy's dairies show that boat drill was a very important feature of life aboard and this discipline instilled in her was possibly to help save her in later adventures. But for the girls at the time, there was a grand social life aboard ship and plenty of opportunities for planned and impromptu concerts and performances. Some of the troops aboard had great talents, especially some Polish officers who sang beautifully. Thus the journey passed very pleasantly and on 10th August, Peggy saw a faint outline of lights on the horizon, her first glimpse of Africa. It seemed extraordinary to see lights glowing freely having come from the dimness of the blackout. She was standing alone on part of the deck in grey slacks, a red jacket and a blue scarf. As the escorting destroyer came alongside, its commander called out that he would like to have that splash of colour on his bridge!

After a final concert and farewell party aboard, the girls disembarked on the 11th August in Freetown, in tremendous rain, where they were met by the ENSA entertainments officer, Captain Philip Madigan. They were installed in a transit camp at Wilberforce which Peggy described at the time in her diary.

"Our quarters are wooden huts with concrete floors and mosquito nets; cold water brought in bowls. Our boy is named Abu and the head boy Sammy. Chop is served in the Transit Cap Mess and is very uninviting"

The orders they were issued with were equally austere and tended to contain dire warnings about everything which could go wrong such as, *"Never leave anything of value or attraction about. Most of the boys will steal and think nothing of it"*, *"Show patience, sometimes you may wait days before being moved"*, *"You are representing ENSA, a name that must be kept fair . . . . never do anything to damage it . . . make your work a duty and a pleasure"*, and perhaps best of all, *"Any person who deliberately attempts to frighten the ladies should be reported"*!

Flies were everywhere in their thousands. The girls quickly learnt to shield their food with their bodies when eating otherwise they would end up eating flies as well as the "chop".

This was a rather unglamorous start to their tour and made worse by the very strict rules and regulations which were imposed on them. They later found out that this was because of fears that they may get into all sorts of trouble. However, once the senior officer, Colonel Haygarth, decided they were five "decent" girls, things relaxed and they were allowed to give their shows and were given much greater freedoms.

(The Five Smart Girls)

(The Five Smart Girls)

The first show in the transit camp was a huge success and afterwards the girls were entertained well by various officers. They gave a concert to the RAF at Fourah Bay and were invited to the Sergeants' Mess. They were the first women to enter this and signed the roll of honour.

The shows followed one another very quickly in camps, aboard ships, in hospitals, all delivered in blistering heat under makeshift awnings or in huts. They were greeted with great enthusiasm wherever they went, but the heat, the pace and the travel were draining for the girls. Peggy found that she ate heartily to gather strength for this, and earned the nicknames of "Panda" and "Small Chop"! The conditions took their toll on the girls who had various illnesses and two succumbed to malaria; at some shows the five girls became three but they improvised, doubled up and never failed to deliver their show—cancelling was simply not an option. Peggy, herself an accomplished pianist, would often take over that role and then have to rush and change for her own number, the violinist could also play the saxophone and so they always managed to put on a good show.

Occasionally there would be a lovely stage such as on the ship "Alcantara". There was a proper stage with lighting and the girls were made very welcome and given an excellent dinner and hospitality afterwards. The Captain generously gave them a huge parcel of tinned food and even eggs and bacon—a rare delicacy—to take away. All was consumed with great relish. So popular were the girls that they were invited back a few days later and gave a shortened version of their show, remaining as guests to watch the rest of the entertainment. Peggy kept the menu card and the letters of appreciation.

No. 40 W.A. General Hospita

September 23th, 1942.

Dear Girls —
            Very many thanks for your letter.
We all thoroughly enjoyed both the grand show
you gave us and the pleasure of entertaining you
afterwards.   We know how trying it must be at
times entertaining under tropical conditions and
we were only too grateful for the opportunity of
showing our appreciation in a practical way.
We only wish there had been more time in which
to give you an even better evening.
            Perhaps, if we are lucky, you
will pass this way again and we shall have a
further opportunity of enjoying your company,
and so whilst keeping our fingers crossed in
anticipation of that happy day, we send you our
very best wishes for your health and safety,
confident that success will attend your worthy
efforts.

            Yours sincerely,

            (Signed) L.W. Davis.

            for "The Boys".

P.S. Pts Walters sends you the words of his
song "Africa" hoping you will have as much fun
out of it as we have.

(Letter of thanks)

Such accolades made any hardships easy to bear.

On 16th October, the girls set out for the Gold Coast by train. Many people turned out to see them off and they were given various presents including a tin of Cadbury's chocolates each. They travelled first class with comfortable armchairs and tables in their carriage but nothing could dispel the terrible dust and the ever oppressive heat. Peggy was fascinated to see that when the train stopped, the Africans would go to the engine and get some water to make a hot drink. They also had no qualms about relieving themselves in full public view by the side of the track. In the absence of any sanitary arrangements on the train, the five girls had to follow suit.

They were met at the other end and given excellent hospitality by their hosts, but this was to be the last comfortable journey for some time as they then had to travel everywhere in an old Ford truck into which were crowded seven people and a piano, and all of their bedding, luggage and basic provisions. They were to travel hundreds of miles in this discomfort but were always enthusiastically greeted by troops and native peoples alike wherever they went, although they presented a sorry sight on arrival anywhere, being covered from head to foot in red dust.

From this time through to the New Year, they embarked on a gruelling schedule of travel and shows and also made the most of all of the social engagements and local events, often not going to bed until 3 or 4 a.m. and then getting on the road again early for the next show. Peggy was fascinated by all of the sights she met and comments in her diary on many of them. At Ju Ju one Sunday she saw the village worshippers walking home from church carrying their bibles on their heads. She loved the rhythmic native dancing and was on several occasions the guest of honour at some of these performances. Once she and an American friend called Morgan danced the Jitterbug to the native rhythm at 2 a.m. surrounded by the villagers dressed beautifully in full evening apparel. It must have been a very comical sight but was very well received! How the women could keep their white finery so perfectly clean in the dust and the climate was a mystery to their visitors who had to work very hard to keep everything presentable.

Things did not always go according to plan. Sometimes they would arrive somewhere to find that no arrangements had been made for them, but kind people always rallied round and even if things went wrong with the performers the show carried on. At an open air show in the 37th Hospital a promised accordionist failed to turn up, their own pianist was ill and so Peggy had to play for everyone else and then stand to do her own acts without music! It really didn't matter. The fact that they were there and providing entertainment was the key thing. It was during this time that Peggy perfected her Snow White, an act developed before the war, where she used unlikely members of her audience to play all of the roles and also her schoolmistress, again engaging with her audience in the front row, all this long before Joyce Grenfall made this type of humour famous. Joyce saw Peggy perform but Peggy's version was very different from the role which Joyce developed later, so there was no rivalry between them. Indeed Joyce and Peggy met on several occasions and Peggy remembers her fondly, particularly admiring her when they met in India and Joyce visited all the hospital wards, spending time with the wounded and bringing them great comfort.

The war in North Africa was hotting up at this time and there was a fear that their area of the Gambia would be bombed and even invaded. Invasion was a real threat, air strikes less so because of the distances involved. The real issue was that the ENSA girls were not in uniform at this stage, and so it was decided that in the event of the warning being sounded for an invasion, Peggy and her friends would go to the native hospital where they would be given nurses' uniforms. They would still be taken prisoner but it was believed they stood greater chances of survival if they were in uniform. Colonel Haygarth gave them a lecture about what to do if bombing and/or invasion occurred. One of the older ENSA ladies wailed that she could not possibly be a nurse as she could not stand the sight of blood!

Huge numbers of troop convoys set off and the social life dwindled rather. At the same time Peggy developed a grumbling appendix but she carried on albeit on a restricted diet, rehearsing throughout most of her 26th birthday and doing a show but still managing to celebrate through to 4am!

The next day they made for Aboekuta in the Nigerian bush where after a quick clean up they performed in a rather grim town hall not only for the local dignitaries but also for the local ruler Ademola II who by that time was about 75 years old. He had done rather well from the British rule and seemed to have negotiated a good salary or pension of some £2500 a year, a very large sum at that time. It is not clear whether he was invited to the performance but it wouldn't have mattered anyway. He had not been invited to the King's coronation but took himself off to London and then the Abbey anyway. These days tight security would have ensured that he got no further, but things were a little more relaxed pre-war and so he attended the ceremony and brought back the stool he used which Peggy saw displayed in his town hall.

The girls were entertained by him which the British consul told them was a great honour. They were also told that as part of the honour they would be presented with a very special gift. They speculated endlessly about what gift Ademola might have for them. Jewellery was the likely thing they felt, but would it be a bracelet, necklace or brooch and with what precious stones? The girls let their imagination run riot. Our man in the area briefed them to do everything the King did and all would be well. Peggy found herself sitting next to the King. They enjoyed a display of wonderful local dancing, vibrant and exciting. It was easy to clap when the King did. The evening wore on and the expected present did not materialise. Then at the very end of the evening it was brought in with much pomp and ceremony—the coveted gift of . . . . a cow!

Clearly this was an awkward diplomatic moment. The girls were due to travel on the next day and a cow did not fit easily with their travel arrangements. The Consul came to their rescue. With the charm and ease of a career diplomat, he explained to the King that, although the girls were delighted and honoured by his generous gift, it simply was impossible for the cow to travel thousands of miles in their cart with them and so regretfully they would be compelled to leave the beast in the King's care.

The King understood and with much ceremony the girls finally left this amazing man's court—and their cow.

Western entertainment and people seemed a little staid for a while after this. Another of the girls, Molly, became ill and had to return to Lagos. Peggy could not accompany her as there were very strict rules on movement at the time due to the "flap" in North Africa.

The month of December was especially busy. With Molly away and feeling ill herself, Peggy's schedule was busier than ever. They gave many performances, visited villages and even a leper colony.

Peggy had of course seen lepers in her childhood and knew that many of the fears about catching leprosy were unfounded. Therefore, she thought nothing of moving amongst the lepers and knelt down and chatted to one group even touching them. They were astonished but delighted.

The group travelled everywhere in their cart with their piano and the best thing of all—a portable loo!

A very crowded Christmas Day kept Peggy active. The girls got up early and went to church, then to an entertainment by native girls; next they served lunch to the men and finally sat down to turkey and Christmas pudding in the mess. They listened to the King's speech and Peggy suddenly felt very homesick. However, she cheered up when she found that the C.O. was Graham Diggens, someone she had known in her teens in Southend.

Eventually the grumbling appendix shouted louder, and in early 1943 Peggy was shipped back to England for its removal.

As she waited to leave, she befriended a young native boy who came to see "white missy" every day. When she got a place on the ship to go home, word spread and, not only the boy, but his Mother too came to say goodbye. The Mother brought a sick baby with her. In very limited English, she pleaded with Peggy to take the baby back to England and make it well. Peggy felt tempted to help but quickly realised that this was not the solution. She took them to the military hospital where the doctor promised to look after the child. It was only a great deal later that Peggy realised that it would have caused much gossip if an ENSA girl had returned home carrying a native child!

Back home

Peggy had her operation and recovered and then joined a concert party in the UK which actually meant a trip to the Hebrides and accommodation in a Nissen hut. The water was supplied by a single tap across a muddy field and the fire wood from the far side of an equally muddy field in the opposite direction. Peggy was also to find that dust was not unique to Africa and that however much you swept dust from a Nissen hut, more dust miraculously appeared to replace it!

It was also freezing cold and on the whole seemed far more unwelcoming than Africa.

Off to Cairo

Having suffered the deprivations of life on the home front, Peggy was eager to travel abroad again. She joined a new group and set off for the Middle East. They were an all women repertory group who were being sent to Cairo with two plays in their repertoire which had been specially written for them. Cairo was where ENSA were making a new base now that Rommel had been driven out of North Africa. The idea was that all costumes would be made and kept there centrally and that all the various travelling groups would go out from there. Ultimately Peggy would help to choose the various costumes, but first of all they had to get to Cairo.

Shipwreck

Peggy joined her new group aboard the ship "Marnix" in the autumn of 1943. On 6th November just as the girls were below deck getting ready for their evening meal they heard and felt a massive explosion. The ship began to list immediately and, although the men on the anti-aircraft guns fired at the planes that had bombed them, the damage was already done. Some crew on the guns were killed and injured, but fortunately for the rest of the ship's company and passengers, the vessel was slow to sink and so everyone was able to take to the lifeboats. The troopship in front of them in the convoy was not so fortunate, neither was one of the accompanying destroyers.

Peggy and her good friends, Kay and Ann, shared a cabin and had been pleased to hear that they were going to be the first convoy to be allowed through the Mediterranean to Egypt for some time. The route was supposed to be safe as Rommel had been chased from the coast of North Africa and the girls were to be spared the long, and sometimes treacherous, journey round the Cape.

However the authorities had not taken into account the Vichy French, who reported the sighting of the convoy to the Germans, who sent out their planes to wreak havoc.

Despite the frightening experience Peggy was immensely proud that not a single woman panicked, whether a QA, WREN or ENSA girl.

They were in the lifeboats for some time and got very wet and cold but were eventually picked up by a destroyer, where they were wrapped in blankets while their clothes dried, and given a delicious hot soup to revive them.

Eventually they were put ashore and ambulances met the QAs, trucks the WRENS and the civilian ENSA artists, who had lost their possessions, were left alone on the quayside, and they had only received half pay during the voyage!

Egypt

The girls were unsure what to do but they were by a huge concrete base that had been laid down by the Germans for their wounded and so they huddled together in this bare place wrapped in a few, somewhat unsavoury, blankets which they had found. The next day a major turned up and they gathered around hopefully. The major made it clear that they were something of a nuisance and that his life would have been made a lot easier if they had all drowned! The men in the companies were extremely angry and the situation became very tense. However, two hours later two lorries arrived and Peggy and the rest of the girls went with the concert party and others to Konstantin. The girls had lost all of their possessions and some were in desperate need of supplies such as sanitary towels and so asked to stop at a chemist, but found to their dismay that the Vichy French refused to serve them.

Worse still, no one seemed to want them but their manager George Dewhurst came to the rescue. George was a true character. He was quite elderly and came from a famous theatrical family, and liked to drink quite a bit, but he could be relied upon in a crisis. He told the girls, "Just keep together and leave it to me" and with that he disappeared leaving them standing in the street. Now they had been forewarned that they should not go into the native quarter, but when George returned he led them into that out of bounds area. They followed with some trepidation to a house where he had arranged accommodation for them—in a brothel! The girls were so grateful that they finally had somewhere clean and comfortable to stay even if they had to share three to a bed top to tail. The "Madame" was a gay young man who spoke English and who looked after them wonderfully well, cooking them delicious meals. It became known in British circles where the girls were and men turned up at the brothel eager to engage the services of the "new girls". Therefore to protect them, the Navy sent two men down to guard them with guns and bayonets! They were, however, much safer there than amongst the Vichy French. They could only go out accompanied by the guards and had to abide by local custom and not walk on the pavement. On one occasion they were able to go with some soldiers to a Disney film. It was planned like a secret mission. They hired a box which hid the girls so no one knew they were there! Peggy's great friend, Kay, fell in love with one of the fellows who took them out. Sadly he worked clearing mines and did not survive the war.

The girls despite having accommodation, albeit 3 to a bed, head to toe, were still very short of the essentials and then one day a Jeep turned up with a sergeant driving. He presented the girls with a holdall full of really useful things, a new guards' uniform which those who were good at sewing made into serviceable clothes for them, handkerchiefs which metamorphosed into bras, pants which could be sewn up to fit girls and joy of joys, rolls of cotton wool which were much needed. All he asked in return was for the holdall back as they were short of such bags! Peggy, however, got permission to go to entertain these wonderful, kind men as a thank you and she gave them her humorous act which was very well received.

(George with the girls)

Finally a boat arrived to take them on the next phase of their journey. It was a troop carrier and conditions were very crowded—two to a bunk this time—but the girls were glad to be on the move again. They were on board on 26th November, Peggy's birthday. One of the girls had saved a brooch from the shipwreck which her husband had given her and she gave it to Peggy, who was hugely touched by such a generous gesture. Peggy has the brooch to this day. She also received a home-made card and the crew sang "Happy Birthday". They were attacked again but not hit, and then when they docked and took the train to Cairo, it derailed. However, to the seasoned veterans of a shipwreck, these things seemed to be merely minor inconveniences.

From this time onwards, as a result of the shipwreck, all ENSA personnel were put into uniform so that if they fell into enemy hands they would be treated as soldiers not spies.

(Peggy and Kay in uniform)

In Cairo, the party were fitted with new costumes and were ready to give their show. The main venue was the Cairo Opera House an amazing wooden building with a brick façade, which in fact was vulnerable to fire so very strict fire precautions had to be put in place. It had been built in the late 1860s and Verdi's opera "Aida" had been written and composed for its opening in 1869. Although a relatively small venue, it was truly beautiful and in spare moments the girls loved to explore the workrooms and wardrobe rooms, admiring them and their contents. The English season opened and the all women cast performed "Ladies in Waiting" which was a thriller. Following this was Ralph Lynne and Tom Walls wonderful farce "It's a Boy". The timing of the production however was not good. King Farouk's wife was expecting a baby and a boy would have caused great rejoicing, but she had a girl. The students went wild and rioted, and tore down the advertising banner, "It's a Boy".

Operating out of Cairo and Alexandria, the girls toured various desert camps where the stages were makeshift. They often were rigged up in haste and there were no luxuries such as wings, so often one had to climb up some rickety steps in full view of the audience, and make an entry with as much dignity as one could muster. It did not matter in the least; the troops were so delighted to be entertained, they did not appear to notice any such shortcomings. The girls also became adept at changing in trailers and tents, often some way from the stage and dealing with their make up in poor or non-existent lighting. There were many ENSA companies working in the Middle East by now and so it was not unusual to bump into someone you knew, and Peggy was delighted to see her old friend from home, David Nixon. They had worked together in concerts and cabaret in Southend, and he was a family friend whom she had known since school days. David had a camera and seemed to have quite a supply of film, unusually in wartime. He loved taking photographs of the people and places he visited, and was as delighted to see Peggy as she was to see him. He took some photographs of her in uniform. He went on to become a household name, but they always remained firm friends, and Peggy was delighted that when his biography was published, not only was she mentioned, but also the photographs he took of her all those years before were included. David sadly did not live to see the launch of his biography, but Peggy went to the launch event and was thrilled to be applauded by the audience.

Throughout the war Peggy kept a diary in which not only did she record the incredible events that she lived through but also her thoughts and feelings—more so as the war progressed. It is very easy, many years later, to imagine that the hectic lifestyle of the ENSA entertainers and their itinerate schedule was endless fun, but after several years of war by 1st January 1944, the stress was beginning to tell. Peggy wrote

"As this is my first entry of the New Year I mustn't sound too depressed—but I can hardly think of a more depressing day . . . . 1943 has proved to be a strange and unforgettable year. I have known the very heights of happiness and the very depths of unhappiness . . . . God give me strength and courage to face the future whatever it may hold for me!"

There was, however little time to dwell on such thoughts as the New Year started with rehearsals and fittings and performances. Unsurprisingly, the group were all tired and tensions ran high. Peggy always found it upsetting when the cast fell out with each other or if some performances were not as polished as they might have been.

On 24th January she noted,

"Mac and Frank came to wish me luck. We needed it!"

Whilst in Cairo, the girls made a publicity film with the same official film unit that had filmed El Alamein. The film, for circulation in cinemas at home, was to show "our boys" on leave with three very proper girls, who were played by Peggy, Kay and Ann. They had a fabulous time visiting the Pyramids and climbing right to the top and riding some beautiful horses. The film was shown at the local cinema in Exmouth and Peggy's Mother got a call from the manager to come and see it.

(Peggy on a camel)

Whilst visiting the Pyramids, Peggy had her fortune told. The fortune teller said she would live another 51 years—a gross underestimate as it happens, but undoubtedly comforting to hear in the midst of war! She was apparently destined to return to Egypt ten years hence, which did not happen, and she was told that several men were in love with her, but she would only love one of them. This certainly proved to be the case as 1944 progressed, but probably true for most of the attractive young women who were engaged in war work in Egypt at that time. In the short term Peggy was more interested in fulfilling her lifelong ambition to ride around the Sphinx on a camel than in pursuing young men.

Thoughts of home were never far away and parcels were always welcomed, but doubly so after the shipwreck. On 9th February, a wonderful parcel arrived with among other things a nightdress and an excellent note in the parcel written by Peggy's Mother to deter any light-fingered handlers. The note said,

"If anyone feels inclined to take any article from this parcel, please think again. This girl is entertaining our boys and last year lost her luggage and now again by torpedo. These things are urgently needed. Thank you. Her Mother."

The parcel not only helped to make things easier, but gave that much valued link with home and buoyed the spirits. Even so, the girls found that there were shortages of some things, and it was a matter for some excitement when Ann kindly gave Peggy some Palmolive shampoo, as the harsh soap she had had to use had made it very difficult for her to maintain a good hairstyle, and of course this was important for someone who was constantly performing.

One of the parishioners at Peggy's Father's church had been killed in North Africa. She asked Mac, who had also been in West Africa, to take her to the cemetery to visit the grave. On the way, they stopped at a florist and Peggy bought a small posy to put on the headstone. When the shop-keeper realised the purpose of the purchase, she gave Peggy armfuls of flowers which she was able to distribute among the rows of temporary crosses. The old caretaker found her an empty tin can to put on the grave she was visiting, and she placed some roses in it. Mac took some very clever photos which made it look as though the whole cemetery was full of flowers. Peggy sent the photos home to the young widow, with the hope that they would afford her some small comfort.

(Mac)

Peggy was also aware of the need to support the troops she entertained, not merely perform and disappear and she noted on 16th February when she stayed to a dance after a show "they were so thrilled that an English girl had stayed behind."

The group then went on to Alexandria where the men had built their own theatre, which was excellent. However, by this time the leading lady was not getting on with the group and elected to leave at very short notice. George came to the rescue and they re-wrote the leading part for a man, but the script had already been learnt and so there were quite a few confusions of "she" and "he" which must have caused some difficulties for the audience, but as ever, people pulled together and the show went on. Peggy was less than impressed when the leading lady was allowed to return and it was this which led her to decide to join a concert party bound for India. Originally she had thought that she may go to Italy as a second front was being opened up but there was a chance to join a 10 handed show called "Happy Go Lucky" bound for India.

However there were still further adventures in Egypt. George knew everyone and made sure that they dined in the finest restaurants—he could always get a table, and he knew all the nightclubs and brothels. He took the girls to meet one

Madame, who sat resplendent in a long black dress with her hair piled high and watched the cabaret. She got on well with Peggy who would often pop in to see her. It was amazing the different friendships one made in wartime!

There were some people, however, who liked to make mischief. Mac met Peggy when she arrived in the Middle East and warned her that some people had started rumours that she had had to leave West Africa because she was pregnant, knowing full well of course that her appendix was the issue. When she met the perpetrators, she endured their effusive hugs and kisses of greetings and then in answer to the question, "How *are* you?" replied that she was very well now thank you, and with perfect timing, left them staring after her as she left with the words "Oh, incidentally, I had twins"!

India

Peggy was excited to be going to India but was sad to leave the many friends she had made in Egypt. They gave her a good send off and Mac gave her "a sweet little lighter" with the inscription *"To Panda from the Nuisance"*. She was also given a Teddy Bear which she christened Teditoo so that he would not be confused with her original Teddy Bear.

(A chance to relax)

They set off for Bombay on 8th March on a little boat with some missionaries and some US airmen, Don and his crew. They were an odd mix of people but they all got on famously. The S.S. Modasa was not a troopship, but a small and not entirely dry passenger ship. Peggy shared a cabin with a girl called Beryl but, understandably nervous after the unceremonious end to her last voyage, she elected to sleep in a deckchair on deck, whilst the ship which was without an escort made way in a zigzag pattern to confound enemy submarines.

They had a jolly time aboard playing cards—Don taught Peggy to play Gin Rummy—, chatting and even dancing. It was a very sociable ship and Peggy noted in her diary some of the jokes the commander told them, for example, "How," he asked, "Do you tell the difference between a legitimate and an illegitimate canary?" There was a pause and then he told them, "You open the cage and the bastards fly out!" This was typical of the light and somewhat juvenile humour which served the purpose of breaking the tension and making people laugh in what could be quite frightening circumstances. Peggy also took solace in the scenery. The views were spectacular and she saw the Southern Cross for the first time.

Blackout had to be observed and on 17th March Peggy confessed to her diary *"For the first time I am really scared"*.

She confided her feelings to Don who was no stranger to the dangers of combat. He agreed that the situation was scary, and indeed said he would rather fly missions than travel on the ship. However convivial they found each other's company, both Don and Peggy were heartily relieved when they sighted Bombay. A corvette then came out to meet them. The harbour was alive with boats and bustling activity. Some people expressed surprise that they had come so far without an escort and reckoned that they had had only a fifty percent chance of getting through especially as their cargo was ammunition and gold!

The American boys had been sent out to drop supplies to support the attack to come. They adopted the ENSA Company like family and vice versa.

They had to go and report for duty but as Don said goodbye, he broke down in tears and presented Peggy with his pilot's large silver wings which he said were his lucky ones. He pledged he would come and visit whenever they could, and for the next few months he was a regular visitor, and Peggy still has Don's wings. They had a close, but platonic, affection for each other. The war, however, took its toll on Don who became an alcoholic. Whenever he came back on leave he would drink heavily. On one leave he came to Peggy and announced "Pegs, I've got religion. Let's go to church". Peggy went with him and on the way he told her that his aircraft had been hit and one of his crew killed. As he limped the plane home he had had to jettison the body and this made him feel very guilty. After they had been to church, he drank a bottle of whisky and continued to drink very heavily. He was invalided home. Peggy realised he now needed drink and so gave the man who was to accompany him home a bottle of whisky with instructions to give him a little at a time. He foolishly handed Don the bottle which was rapidly consumed. Peggy never knew what became of Don, but suspected he died as no one could keep up that rate of alcohol consumption and survive. The war claimed many victims indirectly such as Don. His leaving saddened Peggy but that was in the future.

(Don)

On landing she reported to ENSA. Colonel Eric Dunsford was the officer in charge, but Peggy was delighted to meet up with Jack Hawkins again, who greeted her with enthusiasm, and also several other performers of her acquaintance.

Peggy was tired after the stressful journey and had a bad gum infection which caused her a great deal of pain. As usual the show had to go on and whatever she felt like, she plunged straight into rehearsals. The infection cleared and Jack helped her settle into a hectic social and professional life.

The extremes of India upset Peggy. She also felt guilty in later life that she did not find out more about her "boy" who looked after her so well. She knew he had a family living somewhere behind the compound but in those days it simply was not the done thing for the English to mix with their servants. The poverty was evident everywhere, but for the service personnel and the resident British population, life was very enjoyable. Peggy was distressed to see such sights as a beggar lying unconscious in the street as a dignitary in a magnificent Mercedes drove past. Bodies were collected daily in carts and she saw the huge funeral pyres burning on the banks of the Ganges. She saw poor Indians emaciated and bathing in filthy water while the Botanical Gardens were well watered and the animals in the zoo well fed. It did not do to think too much about the inequalities and anyway there were problems enough for an English girl new to India. The mosquitoes and cockroaches were no respecters of people, and there were many other dangers, such as snakes, to contend with, and just the climate itself was severely debilitating. There were, however, compensations such as a plentiful supply of food and entertainment.

Peggy enjoyed the social whirl and the performances and was particularly glad that when she played a Cockney in the show, a real Cockney sergeant came backstage to ask if she was a true Cockney as she was the first person he had heard since leaving home who "*sounded just like one of us*".

Peggy loved to go sightseeing wherever she was but the grinding poverty did not always make it a pleasant experience.

Don visited when he could and Peggy loved to see him. "What a grand lad", she wrote, but the first hints of his extreme stress were beginning to show, and Peggy worried for him and his crew as a number of their colleagues were posted as missing.

Sleep was a problem in India due to the heat and Peggy was often exhausted particularly when the group had to travel long distances by crowded trains with very poor, and often no, sanitation. The incentive to keep going was that the shows were extremely well received.

During her time in India, Peggy acted as welfare officer for the ENSA artistes, which involved helping them in every way to make their lives run more smoothly, whether it be sorting out accommodation or providing a shoulder to cry on when things went wrong. She also sometimes found herself responsible for making sure some of the stars got to their various venues on time. Some were easier to deal with than others. Gracie Fields, a long established star, insisted on touring to entertain the troops despite still recovering from major surgery. However, she was not always as well received as she might have hoped. Gracie still had a strong and loyal following amongst the young men who had grown up with her famous songs. There were many, however, in England and abroad who disapproved strongly of her Italian born husband, Monty Banks. Peggy remembers him as extremely unpopular and that he told particularly unpleasant and "blue" stories. Gracie suffered the impact of this and once Peggy saw Gracie receive a very poor reception when she sang "Ave Maria" at one concert just after Banks had told some of his unsavoury jokes. Peggy kept her girls well away from the attentions of Mr Banks!

Vera Lynn was a different story. Peggy remembers her performing beautifully in an evening dress, but something was missing. Vera also seemed ill at ease dining with the top brass. Then someone had a brainwave. Vera was sent out in uniform to perform from a Jeep wherever there were soldiers. A mini piano was attached to the Jeep and the driver was the pianist. She had a microphone attached to a dynamo so that she could sing anywhere. The results were magical—the Forces' sweetheart was in her element and the troops adored her.

Some stars caused scandal and trouble. Peggy remembers one incident when a star persuaded a young flying officer to fly her totally illegally to meet her lover, a famous military figure. It was rumoured she used her "charms" to persuade the young man into this action. He was disciplined for the episode, Peggy felt unfairly, and it was decided by the ENSA leaders that the star should be sent home. It gave Peggy great pleasure to escort her to the boat!

Peggy performed regularly with her group known as "The Stop Gaps". They could be sent to perform anywhere at very short notice and were always very popular. It all started when a famous star refused to perform unless she was put into a better hotel. There was none available and so the star stuck to her word and would not perform. Peggy, at very short notice, put on her best frock and provided her "Snow White" and various numbers, her driver did a conjuring act, another helper played the piano and a group of three Indian sisters, who had an act similar to the Andrews sisters, completed the line up. It was a scratch show but a huge success and thereafter, literally filled the gaps when needed.

(Concert Parties)

(Concert Parties)

Peggy, despite a punishing work schedule, always found time for her friends and to enjoy music. One such friend was a young Lieutenant in the Transport unit called Peter, who had a prized possession, a gramophone. Peter had a deep love and great knowledge of classical music which he would play to all of the lads in the unit. At first, the lads were a little sceptical; most were more familiar with the popular music of the day than the classics, but Peter had a unique way of making the beautiful music accessible to all as he would conduct each piece. This he did with such skill and passion that, through his movements, the audience "saw" the orchestra. Peggy was as enthralled by this as the men, and she was soon discussing the music and the background to the pieces with him, impressed by his vast knowledge. After a short while, they developed informal "concerts" in their spare time, where Peggy would introduce a piece of music and talk about such things as the historical context briefly, and then Peter would conduct in his usual mesmerising style. These events became known as "Peter and Peggy", and word got around that this was something worth seeing. Sometimes a few people came to join them in Peter's barracks and sometime the place was packed out. Peggy had had to ask permission from ENSA to do this, but so long as she did it in her spare time, there were no objections, and these enjoyable events gave her great pleasure and provided a welcome break from her busy duties.

The ENSA girls were always in demand for parties and dances and on one occasion Peggy was asked if she and a friend would go to a dance with some badly burnt soldiers who were recovering from their wounds. She knew from her earlier experience at East Grinstead that this would not be an easy task, and so she elected to go with her a girl who would be able to dance with the disfigured men without blanching. They had a wonderful evening and Peggy found herself dancing with one young man whose voice seemed familiar, but whose face was dreadfully damaged. He introduced himself to her as a member of her church at home. She then realised that he had been one of the best looking men that she had ever met. All the girls at church had been in love with him. She smiled and laughed and danced with him and did not let him see her distress at his suffering. The actress as ever put on an excellent performance.

There were other poignant moments too. Once whilst performing at a rehabilitation centre for men wounded' in Burma, in an improvised auditorium, she realised to her horror that her "Snow White" would be highly inappropriate as some of the wounded were paralysed. How could she ask them to wave their handy-pandies and do all the other ridiculous actions?

But it was too late to change the act and so she went ahead. When she reached the waving your handy-pandies bit she saw, slowly and painfully a young man gradually move one finger and then another and smile. Afterwards he thanked her. She was then told it was the first time he had moved his hands since being injured. She felt like weeping but kept the bright smile firmly fixed in place.

Peggy did not lack for male company during this time but only wanted friendships with the men she met, and she valued such people as Bill Sykes, about whom she wrote, *"He is a grand person one of the few who treats me as I like to be treated—as a pal—no lines—no strings"*. She valued talking to him and found they had much in common, and she loved the silk scarf he gave her made from parachute silk. With some other men, she found life not so easy and sometimes had to remind them that she was a married woman!

Tigers

Peggy had little time for relaxation in India with her own performances and her welfare role but she still enjoyed invitations to dinner and social events.

At one she met the director of the Tatanagor Steelworks, Bill Blundell, who had two pet tigers. He was an American who had lived for some years in India. Peggy was invited with the people she was staying with at the time to come to brunch. Knowing he had these beautiful tigers, it was an invitation which the animal loving Peggy accepted without hesitation. Her hosts took her to brunch. Peggy was sitting on the veranda and the tigers came into the compound coupled together by a long lead. Peggy had always loved tigers and indeed had played with tiger cubs at London Zoo when she was Baby Peggy. She was not remotely afraid of them so she went to stroke them with absolutely no problems. Bill was thrilled that she had such a rapport with the animals and she returned over several days and got to know the animals well.

On the day she was due to leave, Peggy had the opportunity to pose for photographs with the tigers. This was an opportunity she did not want to miss. However, Peggy had started her period, a fact she conveniently "forgot" to mention. All appeared to be well and the photographs were duly taken, but then the male tiger instinctively pounced, mauling her right arm quite badly inflicting a total of 17 wounds on arms and legs. The shocked onlookers wanted to put iodine on the wounds but Peggy remembered her Mother always advised to flush out wounds with water.

She was therefore sluiced down with buckets of water. She was rushed to hospital, carried on a stretcher by two Ghurkhas, and still carries the scars to this day. News of the attack reached the ENSA C.O., Colonel Dunstan, who was with Noel Coward at the time.

"Good grief, Noel," he said, "one of my gels has been mauled by a tiger".

"During the performance?" quipped Coward.

Peggy was saddened that the tiger had to be destroyed and she had to stay in hospital for a while where the only treatment was washing the wound with carbolic and hoping for the best. Fortunately the treatment worked, but it was a long recovery. It is interesting that Peggy had noted in her diary the day before the attack that the tigers were *"getting out of hand"*. But she had not expected an attack!

After two days in hospital Peggy signed herself out as she felt she could not miss too many shows, but she had to return daily for dressings until eventually the arm was plastered, giving her a little more freedom. She found herself to be something of a celebrity, but felt very low and homesick. She was not a good patient *"how hateful it is to be dependent on others "*, she wrote, an attitude she has maintained throughout life. Others in the company were also suffering from various illnesses largely due to the heat and associated problems, so the whole company was given 2 weeks' leave from 6th June. It was only afterwards they heard that this was indeed a special day—D Day. Peggy enjoyed the break and the group celebrated her wedding anniversary. Peggy wrote, *"goodness knows what I have to celebrate but still!"* It was great to have a party whatever the reason!

(Peggy with the tigers just before the attack)

The bureaucrats had heard of the tiger attack and a memo was sent out to all ENSA company managers saying that artistes would in future have to be personally responsible for any injuries incurred if they participated in a long list of activities such as swimming, riding and at the end of the list came "playing with tigers"! Even in the midst of war, health and safety and legal minefields still had to be negotiated!

On 30th June Peggy met a man who was to have a profound effect upon her, Guy Randel—(see chapter on Men at War).

At the same time that Peggy enjoyed her great romance with Guy, she was still living life to the full with ENSA and looking out for poor Don. She suffered bouts of ill health herself and had to spend a few days in hospital with a high temperature. Don drank to excess during this time but was ashamed of himself afterwards, and bought Peggy a beautiful wristwatch as an apology. He vowed to keep sober but could not.

Peggy continued to enjoy sightseeing in her rare time off and visited a beautiful carved marble mausoleum where she bought a little marble rabbit as a souvenir. These outings were quite rare as the days were filled with costume fittings, rehearsals and travel and make up arrangements, not to mention the performances and the welfare work, all in the extreme heat and with the ever present mosquitoes making life uncomfortable to say the least.

Things did not always go smoothly. Once, the wagon with all the costumes was mistakenly unhitched from their train during the night. The cast arrived but nothing else. They could never cancel and let down the troops and so eventually they got enough together to put on a late show which started at 10.45pm.

Hospital shows were always poignant and Peggy was moved by one boy who was paralysed and temporarily out of an iron lung for the first time to see the show. On other occasions, however tired she was, she led the others to speak to the wounded after a show.

On September 1st she was performing as usual and doing her Snow White routine. As usual, she cast a member of the audience as Snow White. She always chose the most unlikely candidate, someone who looked quite tough. On this occasion, she picked a young RAF officer whom she noted to be *"a nice type"*.

The "nice type" contacted her the next day and asked her to meet him. His name she found out was Arthur Clegg and that meeting would ultimately change her life—he fell in love as soon as he saw Peggy—(see chapters on Men at War and Arthur Again).

Peggy performed for all of the various dignitaries who came to visit the troops and no one was safe during "Snow White". Brigadier Slim himself came to open a rest and recuperation centre set up for the men as they came out of the line known as the Nip Inn. He found himself cast in the leading role, a situation which he took in good part, much to the delight of his men!

At the beginning of 1945, despite her own illness, her worry over the men in her life and her busy welfare role, Peggy returned to rehearsals and shows. She had a job to do and was determined to do it and do it well. She had flowers from Vic, a note of encouragement from Jack Hawkins and a letter from Guy, all helping to give her the energy to work on.

Indeed Jack Hawkins was so impressed with her that he invited her to join a party to go to Ceylon.

At that stage in the war, famous performers were coming out to India and Peggy met George Formby whom she described as *"a delightful man and I feel at home with him straight away"*

At the beginning of March, Jack Hawkins asked her whether she wanted to continue in welfare or be an artist; *"be an artist"* was the immediate reply, but for a while after the two roles had to continue and Peggy found herself so busy that in the last few months of the war her diary was fragmented.

The end of the war

At the end of the war Peggy came home in uniform. She had stayed on to go to Rangoon to open a small ENSA centre there but she had become very ill after picking up a bug via a mosquito bite which attacked her face and teeth. She was very sad not to see the final job through. She had set up all that was needed to go to the new centre and had it packed up into the pontoon ready to be transported, everything from office furniture to costumes, but they had to sail without her. There was an element of relief, however, to be leaving the punishing climate.

Peggy sailed home on the "Mauritania" accompanied by many Anglo-Indian and Indian girls who had married

British men during the war and were coming to Britain to an unknown life. Many were not prepared for either the climate or the suspicious reception they were likely to receive in some areas. In some cases the men folk, who had promised much, had apparently disappeared. Peggy felt sorry for the girls but her own future was also far from assured, but at least she had the support of her ever loving parents and as she was not fit enough to stay in ENSA she returned home to Devon to recuperate. She had to go for treatment to the Tropical Diseases Hospital in London and lost her back teeth to the infection, but it eventually cleared up.

CHAPTER 5

MEN AT WAR

Admirers

During wartime, danger and uncertainty tends to lead to some very special and intense relationships and Peggy was certainly not short of admirers! However she regarded most of the men she met as friends rather than in a romantic light and she enjoyed light hearted flirting and much laughter with many. There were some young men who hoped for more. One, in West Africa, took her for a walk in the evening through some long grass. He carried some cushions in hope but Peggy, blissfully unaware of his intentions, announced that she hated walking through the long grass. He looked deeply disappointed and the penny dropped. Peggy roared with laughter and so did he. They remained firm friends.

There were poignant moments too. One officer, Frank Wastell, was due to take Peggy out to dinner. He asked if he could arrive early and watch her do her hair and put her make up on. She agreed, although a little puzzled. He sat in rapt silence watching her as she went through her make up ritual in front of the mirror. Afterwards he thanked her and said he had been imagining his wife doing the same at home. Peggy was touched by this and considered it a privilege to be able to help someone cope with the privations and loneliness of war in this way.

There was heartbreak too. Many of the young men Peggy befriended would not survive the war, and she had to comfort others in the ENSA groups who lost people close to them too. It was not until relatively recently reading around the subject again that Peggy truly appreciated the terrible conditions many of her close male friends had to suffer. They did not talk about it and, unsurprisingly, sought distraction in the social life around them whilst on leave.

Vic

Wartime romances were commonplace and many hasty marriages were entered into when call up papers came. Such marriages were often mistakes to be regretted later.

Peggy found herself in just such a situation soon after the war began.

She had met Vic a few years previously on a trip to Bruges with her friend Audrey. The two girls met and became friendly with two Welsh boys, one of whom was Vic. Boys at this point held no real interest for Peggy, and indeed she had never kissed a boy. Vic, however, appealed to the musician in her, as he had the most beautiful tenor voice she had ever heard. If she did not fall in love with the man, she certainly fell in love with the voice. Peggy kept a notebook of the visit and filled it with photographs and details of all of the beautiful places she visited. "I played for Vic Jones (tenor)" is the only mention of him however. Vic's friend cautioned her that this was merely a holiday romance and should not be taken too seriously, but the relationship continued. Peggy and Vic corresponded regularly and she sent him songs on his birthday. Tenors invariably sing love songs and the songs she sent therefore may have sent out stronger messages than were meant. Vic came to sing at Peggy's 21st birthday party and again the nature of the songs gave their relationship a strong air of romance.

Prince Karl Franz
MR. V. P. JONES

(Vic as the Student Prince)

Peggy was invited to stay with his family in the Rhondda one Christmas and had the most wonderful time. She disliked the area as everything was covered in coal dust, but everyone was welcoming and friendly and she received a lovely pink handbag as a Christmas present which soon changed colour with the dust.

Vic was illegitimate which was still a social stigma in those days, and he was very aware of this. Peggy regarded such things as totally unimportant and realises with hindsight that she had, in fact, been leading Vic on for some time into believing their relationship was deeper than it was.

Vic was a house tutor at Loughborough College, where he taught Art, and was leading tenor in the Operatic Society. Theirs was therefore a distance relationship, but war was to change all that.

When Vic received his call up papers for the RAF, he immediately phoned Peggy and asked, "Will you marry me?"

Peggy's instant reaction was to say "no", and Vic's instant response was that she was refusing because he was illegitimate. Peggy then, with characteristic spontaneity, changed her answer to "yes" to disprove the point.

Things moved on very quickly from that moment. The very next day, Peggy went to meet Vic at Swan and Edgar's tearoom in London where he presented her with an engagement ring, to which she took an instant dislike. At home her Mother was making hasty wedding arrangements including the full bridal regalia and bridesmaids, and Peggy, although knowing it was all a mistake, went along with it all. Soon she was at the door of the church on her Father's arm. Years later, her Father said that there in the porch of the church, he nearly asked her if she wanted to call the whole thing off, as he had misgivings as to whether this was right for Peggy.

However, no words of protest were uttered by anyone and a few minutes later Peggy found herself a married woman, Mrs Jones. Her Father paid for them to spend a one night honeymoon in a hotel. Peggy pretended she had her period and so Vic went off to war and the marriage was not consummated. It was never to be consummated. Not only did Peggy know that she had made a mistake in marrying Vic but she also found the concept of a sexual relationship with anyone abhorrent. She feared a physical relationship because she had seen the devastating effect of childbirth and successive miscarriages on her Mother's health, which not only had a major effect on Peggy's childhood, but was to have a significant bearing on the whole of her adult life.

Vic served in the RAF and was first stationed in Blackpool and Peggy was abroad with ENSA. Peggy confessed in a letter to Guy later in the war that one of her main motives for accepting a posting abroad was to escape dealing with the issue of her marriage. Even when Vic and Peggy had a short leave together in Blackpool, she contrived to be recalled and thus avoided the thorny subject of sex again. But this state of affairs could not continue.

Towards the end of October 1944, Peggy heard from Vic that he had been given some leave. They both thought that this must be embarkation leave and Peggy expected that he would be sent to France. However, at the beginning of November, she learnt that he was in fact being sent to India. *"What now?"* she wrote with some trepidation.

They met on December 16th when he arrived in India, *"not a happy meeting, I am afraid"* she recorded. After a few tense days, Peggy had no choice but to be honest with him. They agreed that they would remain married in name only, which Peggy said was a great weight off her mind, but even so the stress of the situation was too much for her.

She had suffered a breakdown and after a spell in hospital had stayed with the Savage family who gave her an apartment of her own and she had time to think about the future. They could not understand why she was not delighted to see her husband when he arrived and neither could Vic. He had no idea how to handle the situation and was unsurprisingly hurt and resentful. Although they met many times over the next few weeks, they continually fell out. On 12th January 1945, she wrote, *"I have shed more tears over Vic than anything else, or perhaps I should say because of Vic"*. Peggy hated the fact that they were *"killing off any remnant of affection"*, and even his beautiful singing voice no longer thrilled her.

Peggy had worried how her parents would react to the concept of their daughter ending her marriage, but she need not have worried. This very special couple showed none of the shock or outrage one may have expected from their generation and supported their daughter without reservation, making the whole unhappy business much easier for Peggy to bear.

At the end of the war the marriage ended and Vic went on to marry a Wren he had met during the war and they had two sons. Peggy was pleased for him and pleased that he had the relationship and family that he had always wanted. Her own issues were not as easy to resolve.

Guy

The great love of Peggy's life was Guy Randel whom she met in India on 30th June 1944. Unfortunately, she met him a little too late in the war. He had been injured earlier in Italy and had fallen in love, or so he thought, with his nurse. Although she was some years older than he, they had very soon married. However, once he met Peggy, he realised that she was his soul-mate and she immediately felt the same.

They met at a dance; Peggy found him enormously attractive, particularly his moustache. He invited her to another dance the following Wednesday. Peggy was wary at first, but by the Monday she had found out a bit about him and determined to go. It was nearly a disaster as Guy was late but happily he arrived just in time and they had a wonderful evening. They shared a similar sense of humour and so began the romance.

(Guy)

With the speed and intensity of wartime romances, things moved quickly and on 7th July Peggy wrote

"God I am lucky to meet someone like Guy—guess Lucky is my middle name—but we seem to think the same thoughts, like the same things and above all have the great gift of being able to laugh together".

Guy was on leave due to illness, but this was due to come to an end very soon, so they made the most of their time together. Illness indeed was to dog him for the rest of his days. He suffered from jaundice and liver damage. Guy loved to buy Peggy gifts which included a lovely little cigarette case engraved *"with love from Guy Darjeeling 1944"* on one side and *"Peggy"* on the other. When Guy returned to his unit, Peggy felt very lonely. The intensity of their love is apparent in her diary . . . *"We have been inseparable for a week".*

At this point the hundreds of letters which they sent each other began. This unique record of their correspondence, their love, their hopes and fears, remains intact today and in their entirety would make a book of their own. These letters reveal a love affair played out against a background of war, when two busy people were required to do their duty, in his case often in extreme danger in Burma, in her case on a busy schedule, and they spent what spare moments they had longing to be together and valuing what time they could snatch together. The letters are tender, amusing and sometimes quite mundane but they reveal a need to communicate with each other as often as possible, and Peggy in particular often wrote more than one long letter in a day. She often sent long accounts of what she had been doing, but more importantly, poured out her love in the pages, often finishing with the words of one of "their" songs with her own spelling to capture the true sound, *"I love you—"and I jest cahnt hep it!""*

She signed herself "Panda" or "Pan" on many occasions, the affectionate nickname first coined in West Africa, and she would imagine herself to be in a special world with Guy.

Guy's letters equally show an intensity of feeling. On 15th July he wrote *"Darling Panda (what a lovely sound that makes—I'll say it again and again "Panda Darling")"*

Later he said, *"I am writing this letter not because I have any news but because I want for a few minutes private communion with you and a letter is the only way now"*.

How difficult it must have been for this young man in the midst of the dangers of war to shut out what was happening around him and to write these sincere and loving letters, but equally how important for him to have his moments of escape too. Some of the difficulties and depravations of war are mentioned in his letters, such as the joy of having a hot bath after a long time in battle, but generally he makes light of such matters and his letters are amusing and chatty. He makes loving comments but these are very often underplayed. Guy would undoubtedly have been aware of the censors reading his missives. He had to content himself with writing such things as

"Oh to see those wicked blue eyes again and to hear an honest laugh".

However, there were times when he threw caution to the wind and wrote,

"I should have the strength of mind to maintain my rigid principles and be politely formal—but I can't. I love you too much Panda, to remain mute in view of your sweet letter. I say it again I love you so much, Panda darling".

Letters were often delayed which caused anxiety to both Peggy and Guy and several would then arrive together, which cheered up the recipient enormously. Guy spoke of working himself into a frenzy every day, wondering if there would be a letter in the post and of blessed relief or agonising disappointment. Some of the correspondence is of necessity fragmented as letters crossed and news was repeated.

Guy also included in many of his letters some pencil drawings and poems, all of which entranced Peggy.

Throughout the difficult year when Guy was often away on missions and she was deeply involved with her ENSA work, they spent time together whenever they could and when apart they wrote to each other constantly. Their relationship was acknowledged and accepted by those around them and Guy was even given leave to spend some time with Peggy before the major battle of Kohima. The CO warned him that a key battle was to come and sent him on leave to see Peggy, adding to give her all their love, so important was she to the lives of many soldiers in the 2nd Div. It had been the practice for many of Guy's friends and colleagues to drop in to see Peggy when on a short leave.

Guy was not, however, in the best of health and had suffered repeatedly from severe jaundice. The illness could affect his moods, something which Peggy did not fully understand at first. It was Arthur who explained the consequences of such an illness, even though he was jealous of the relationship.

When Guy arrived on leave in mid September, Peggy was overjoyed. She had been fearful she would not feel the same way when she actually saw him but the romance continued to blossom, and they danced and enjoyed a brief few days together before his leave was cut short and he had to return to duty. However, he just had time to order a cross-keys brooch for her, his division's emblem. Guy continued to struggle with illness but would not let it mar his leave. It was 11ᵗʰ November before they would meet again but the loving correspondence continued. Peggy had written to say she was likely to return home and Guy was granted leave to dissuade her. He watched her perform for the first time from the wings and she wrote, "Heaven indeed to be loved like this".

Peggy determined to stay on.

Their love deepened in this all too short leave and they desperately wanted to have a future together, although deep down both knew this was unlikely.

Life was complicated by Vic's arrival in India and the pulls of professional and private obligations.

Peggy wrote in her diary in January 1945 *"What am I to do? The only future I want is to be Guy's wife, look after his home, bear his children. If that is to be denied me, what can fate have planned as a substitute?"*

By mid May Peggy sensed that there was something amiss with the relationship. On his brief leaves, she tried so hard to please him but found that she often irritated him instead; even her plans for a romantic celebration of his birthday fell flat. This was undoubtedly due to his deteriorating health and on 30th May he was admitted to hospital for many weeks. He told Peggy not to *"make an institution of visiting"* and he was adamant that she must not put her career in jeopardy on his account. Her love remained undiminished, but she wondered if he was trying to let her down gently, as he would soon be returning to England and his wife. On June 10th a repatriation scheme was announced for the sick and wounded. Guy would undoubtedly qualify for this. Peggy was torn between a desire to go home herself and to go on to further work with ENSA. In the end, her own ill health was the deciding factor.

As late as August 1945, Peggy and Guy were still writing to each other virtually daily but there was increasing tension between them as the war drew to a close and a return to civilian life beckoned. The love clearly was still strong, but the complexities of their situation were equally so.

At the end of the war there was to be no happy ending for Guy and Peggy.

He returned her letters to her at her request for safekeeping, which she kept along with the ones she received from him, and returned to his wife.

Peggy did not expect to see him again, although she thought of him a great deal, but a chance encounter in London rekindled a flame and Guy contacted her Father to obtain Peggy's telephone number. They kept in touch, meeting discreetly from time to time. Peggy knew instinctively when the phone rang that it was Guy calling. Her secretary used to tell her if she was not around that that "dark brown voice" had called. Guy's health remained poor during this time, but Peggy did not realise just how poor. One day she missed a call from him and expected him to call again but he did not. She never phoned his home and was anxious not to cause him any difficulties but as time passed, she worried about him greatly. She was doing an examining job in his home town and called his home number from a phone box. A woman, presumably his wife, answered and Peggy asked politely if she could speak to Mr Randel.

"He's dead," was the brusque response.

Peggy put the phone down shocked and heartbroken. With hindsight, she felt his final call may have been to say goodbye from hospital and she deeply regretted that they did not have the opportunity for the final farewell. Her "dark brown voice" was no more.

However, ever with a great sense of responsibility, Peggy pulled herself together to do the examining job. The show still had to go on.

Arthur

On 1st September 1944, Peggy gave a performance and did her Snow White routine. This involved casting unlikely members of the audience in unlikely roles. By chance there was a young RAF officer in the audience whom she chose to be Snow White, much to the amusement of his colleagues who ragged him about it for days. Peggy noted in her diary that he was *"a nice type"*.

She learned that his name was Arthur Clegg and he was a Squadron Leader with the Dental Corps. The very next day, he asked her to meet him.

Although much of her time and love interest was focussed on Guy, Arthur and Peggy were also much drawn to each other. They had dinner together virtually daily, and after two weeks he declared he was in love with her.

Arthur knew of Guy's existence and the special relationship Peggy enjoyed with him, but he, nonetheless, continued to love Peggy, and she grew ever more fond of him. She noted in her diary that he was always very attentive, and *"Also he is so sweet about Guy's possible arrival"*

He looked after her with tenderness and dedication when she was ill, and they spent time together whenever they could.

Peggy, unsurprisingly, *"got the jitters"* when they were out together and she saw a tiger at the zoo. Arthur was very understanding and helped her through the difficult situation. He helped to dispel her fears and nightmares. She wrote *"AC has really fallen in love with me. Must admit he is a delightful companion and I am very fond of him"*

Peggy found sleep increasingly difficult and was becoming more and more exhausted. On more than one occasion Arthur sat with her until she fell asleep, which she found easier in his calming presence.

She expected when they parted on 18th September that she would not see him again and he gave her at the end of *"such a happy last evening together"* several presents, including a lovely little photograph of himself in a silver frame.

(Arthur in India)

(Arthur in India)

The next day Peggy wrote sadly, *"7.30 seemed very strange—no Arthur arriving—miss him far more than I thought"*

In fact, they were very soon together again and he looked after her when she had a fever.

Peggy and Arthur corresponded regularly, but at the end of the war parted reluctantly. Arthur re-read Peggy's letters on the boat home and then tore them up and threw them into the water. He believed that he had someone waiting for him at home, but that proved not to be the case. He went on to marry his theatre nurse and have a family, but still had a great fondness for Peggy.

Peggy kept all of her correspondence from Arthur. They are well written, chatty letters full of news but always expressing his love for his "sweetest Pegs". Many start with *"my darling"* and he told her she made him feel *"all good inside"*, a phrase she had used about him.

In January 1945 he was writing, *"I am still very much in love with you"* and he knew that *"September in Lahore was a phase I shall always be able to re-live for the rest of my days"*.

He sent her poems and cards and continued to correspond after the war.

They met in London on several occasions, but very properly had separate rooms. Arthur continued to build a successful career in the RAF. At breakfast during one of these meetings, a colleague of Arthur's, coincidentally staying in the same hotel, came to talk to him. Thinking quickly, Arthur pretended that he had just met Peggy as a fellow lone visitor and had asked her to join him for breakfast.

"I am sorry I don't know your name," he said to her.

"Peggy" she replied sweetly, but with a heavy heart as she knew that this was evidence that her continuing to meet Arthur, however chastely, could undermine his career if there was any breath of scandal, and so they agreed that they would not see each other again. Life was very different in that post-war era compared with today, and indiscretions were not forgiven. It was a difficult decision, but they both pursued their careers with enthusiasm, Arthur rising to high rank in the RAF and Peggy in performing and in teaching, ultimately owning her own school. He kept her photographs and she his but they never expected to see each other again.

CHAPTER 6

BUILDING A CAREER AFTER THE WAR

West of England Theatre Company

Peggy returned to health on her return home after the war, and one day received a call from Joyce Worsley who was starting a company in the Devon area with support from the Arts Council. It was to be called "The West of England Theatre Company. She invited Peggy to audition in London. The audition required that she read from J.B. Priestley's "They Came To A City". Priestley himself was at the audition and remained utterly expressionless, but Peggy was invited to stay behind and read more, apparently impressing Priestley. This performance led to the forging of a good relationship and over the years Peggy appeared in many of his plays.

Life with the Company was good and very busy and revolved around the Company's base, a house in Exmouth where everyone worked hard, but the Company ran on a very small budget. There were never any understudies and at one point Peggy had to be carried to the wings of the stage with a broken leg! At first they travelled around in an old van which regularly broke down and on more than one occasion Peggy's Father and other friends had to come to rescue them. Peggy had the opportunity to act in "Blithe Spirit" in the role of Ruth. She received very positive commendations for this role. R.F. Delderfield wrote *"Excellent in every way. It would be difficult to over estimate the degree of assurance with which that unsympathetic role was handled. One of her greatest assets is the clarity of her diction."* She also appeared in "Macbeth" and "The Dover Road" by A.A. Milne to name but a few. The roles brought many more positive reviews particularly the role of Eustasia in "The Dover Road" in which not only did she make the audience laugh but Delderfield wrote, *"Her floods of tears were among the most realistic I have ever witnessed and her study of the spoilt and vapid woman is further proof of her remarkable versatility"*.

The programmes reveal that the shows came rapidly one after another. This required her learning lines for one play, rehearsing another and performing in a third as she had had to in rep before the war. It was hard work. They were however happy and fulfilling days.

<u>BBC</u>

After two years Peggy had the chance to go to London to do "Scrapbook of 1925" where she was interviewed about her role as Baby Peggy. She found many opportunities to pick up various parts at the BBC by lunching at the BBC Club, which had a great family atmosphere in those days. Sunday Afternoon Theatre was one of the most popular programmes of the day and Peggy regularly got parts in these. She even did a show with the great heart throb Douglas Fairbanks Jnr, in which she had a role as a young London girl, feeding him lines to talk about London. This was not a fully scripted piece—he just picked up the lead and talked, so it was all rather nerve racking but actually turned out very well.

There were also parts in popular series such as Dick Barton, where she was part of the original cast for about six months, and Mrs Dale's Diary, in which she played the Dales' son's girlfriend for several months; these programmes were highly popular in their heyday.

Peggy had several moments when she thought her hoped for big break had come. Cochrane liked her work after he interviewed her for the Scrapbook and he had links with the great impresarios of the day. He promised her work, but sadly died before anything could happen.

Then Tommy Handley decided that he needed a new voice in his hit show, ITMA ("It's That Man Again"). Peggy went with many hopefuls for the first audition, and then was recalled for a second. At the third audition there were just two contenders, Peggy and a man. This time Handley himself was there. Peggy read from a script with Handley and at the end of it she was told she would be the new voice in ITMA. She was asked to the next recording to meet everyone and had a wonderful time. To be in ITMA meant that she had really arrived and, after a short summer break, they were due to start recording the new shows. Peggy went on holiday very excited and went out to dinner with some friends, who had the wireless on in the background. It was there she heard the devastating news that Tommy Handley had died. The big career break never happened and, instead of a secure future, she was back to picking up work on an ad hoc basis at the BBC. She was never out of work in this period, but it was an uncertain life, although one she relished.

Wembley again

In 1948, Britain, war torn and impoverished, hosted the Olympic Games, largely because no one else wanted to or was in a position to do so. There was no massive new building programme for this, as all available money and resources were still going into rebuilding the shattered cities, and so the games centred around the place where Peggy had first made her mark, Wembley.

This time the BBC played a large part in the event, not only by commentating on the various competitions, but they also held interviews with the many successful athletes from all over the world. To put on a protracted outside broadcast of this type required many people from the BBC, and Peggy worked throughout the games co-ordinating the athletes, interviewers and technicians. It was difficult to get everyone in the right place at the right time and there was no margin for error. It was exciting work and she got to see most of the most famous athletes of the day as well as the thrill of the live broadcast work, still a nerve racking process today, but doubly so in the days of fairly basic equipment.

It required good organisational skills to get the right people to the right place at the right time, and when the games were over Peggy found herself doing some administrative work at the BBC as well as continuing to broadcast. She was then asked to run a new department to organise similar broadcasts of outside events, such as the Royal Horse Show. This would have been a "proper" job with a regular salary and a secure future and indeed an interesting role, but Peggy in her usual impetuous way did not think about it, and said she wanted to be a performer not work in an office. Peggy also rather ruined her chances with the BBC by accepting a summer tour with the company "Gaytime", including among others, rising star, Benny Hill.

(Benny Hill)

It was great fun to be on the road again and Peggy loved the performances but at the end of the summer the work dried up.

What she didn't realise was that in those days there was no such thing as a second chance with the BBC and this marked the end of her broadcasting career for a very long time.

Throwing it all away

Throughout the post-war period, Peggy had also been involved with teaching, adjudication and examining work. This worked quite well alongside the irregular performance work and made it possible for Peggy to earn a living. She was not an actress who "rested"

She was lucky enough to be introduced to Peter Browne, a highly successful agent who only took a few people on to his books, and never more than one of any type of performer. He wanted to represent Peggy but she also was continuing with her work examining for Guildhall. He found her roles in the new black and white TV series such as Emergency Ward 10 and various thrillers.

One day on the way through London to an examining job, she used a red telephone box at the station to call him as requested. He told her he had a role lined up for her, which required her to start immediately. Peggy explained that she had an examining commitment. He growled that she must decide whether she was working for Guildhall or pursuing an acting career with him. At her most impetuous and without any real thought, Peggy said she must fulfil her Guildhall commitment. There was no going back. He never answered any further calls from her and the work dried up completely. This is the moment that Peggy looks back on with the most regret, the moment when she says she "threw it all away." She feels sure that if only she had made the opposite decision at that moment, her world would have changed forever and she would have gone on to achieve so much more in the world of entertainment.

CHAPTER 7

EDUCATING OTHERS

At her most depressed, Peggy finds it hard to understand that, whereas this defining moment in the red telephone box may have cost her performing career, it opened the way for her to throw herself wholeheartedly into the world of education, and thus have a profound and lasting influence on many performers and individuals in all walks of life. There are many performers who will not go on stage without first blowing their noses and "spending a penny", so much was this drilled into them by the formidable Miss Batchelor, as well as a wealth of performance skills! The handwritten notes for the Associate teaching course continued to be circulated by pupils at Tring Park School (then known as The Arts Educational School, Tring) for a good ten years after Peggy left, so clear and thorough were they. It is no surprise that many, many past pupils keep in touch and that still, at the age of 95, she has a few pupils.

She taught many children at a theatre club at the Questors Theatre in Ealing, including some who were to go on to be household names. Dusty Springfield was a difficult pupil, but hugely talented, and Peggy was not at all surprised that her career took off. She followed her career with great interest, as she was to do for many other pupils over the years, but she was saddened that Dusty did not have the happiness to match her success, and she mourned the premature death of her famous pupil.

She delights to see past pupils on stage and large and small screen and derives great joy from watching them do well. The work of young performers such as Amy Nuttall and Bryony Hannah who were pupils thrill her and her influence is evident in their clear diction.

Ridley School and Studios

Peggy realised that she would have to gain a teaching diploma to pursue a career in education fully and so she returned to Guildhall. Whilst there her tutor, Guy Pertwee, invited her to join a new organisation of which he was co-founder, The Society of Teachers of Speech and Drama, and so in 1952, Peggy attended the inaugural meeting and ultimately became the Society's Chairman.

But that was in the future. Peggy began teaching in earnest, including working at the prestigious Guildhall and on something of an impulse decided to start a school of her own in a beautiful building with which she fell in love at Leigh-on-Sea. In 1955 the Ridley School and Studios opened and over the years, thrived. Peggy called on old friends to be patrons, such as Dame Sybil Thorndike, Dame Peggy Ashcroft and Jack Hawkins.

The press cuttings of the time, carefully cut out and put into scrapbooks by Peggy's Mother, show that the School went from success to success. Not only did the School put on excellent productions, usually directed by Peggy, but individual pupils achieved successes in festivals and competitions, and some went on to a career in the performing arts.

The high point of life at the Ridley Studios was its 21st birthday celebrations.

The pavilion was hired and filled with about 1,000 people. The Mayor and all the local dignitaries were present and the School showed itself at its best. The Head Boy and Head Girl gave a history of the School and messages of congratulations were read from Dame Sybil Thorndike and the other patrons. A wonderful performance then took place, which Peggy directed, called "21 Not Out". It was a "Kaleidoscope of Entertainment", ranging from Mozart to "The Sound of Music", with speech, with dance and a dazzling array of acts. Peggy was so proud of all of her pupils and so pleased at the recognition of the work in which she believed so passionately. Ridley Studios provided tuition in every genre of the performing arts and tutors came from London to teach and take workshops. It was not a place to clone "little stars" but to teach the skills of performance and to encourage each child to give of their best.

It was during this period of her life that Peggy also found time to travel abroad again and in the 1960s went on special excursions organised by John Letts, often at quite short notice. These tours tended to be theme based, perhaps on some particular period of History or aspect of the country's culture, and the guides were always expert and excellent.

In this way Peggy went to Russia at a few days' notice. Peggy knew nothing about what was to happen, but just turned up at the airport and got on the plane. She found herself alone at Moscow Airport as no one appeared to meet her. She passed the time with a ticket collector who looked incredibly like George V. Although Peggy spoke no Russian and he spoke no English, they got on famously, especially when she showed him an English coin with the late King's head on it. She was quite disappointed when her escort finally arrived! She and the other guests in the small group were taken to the very basic National Hotel and from there were taken on bus tours. Those were interesting, but Peggy preferred it when she communicated with local people. Her camera went wrong and she managed to take it to a repair shop, where everyone crowded round to see the visitor. Sign language is universal, and with smiles and nods, the camera was taken away and mended perfectly. However, the shopkeeper refused payment. They just seemed so pleased to see a tourist, as this was still a new concept in just post-Stalinist Russia.

The party went on to Leningrad and this time stayed in a magnificent, purpose built hotel, overlooking the river. One of the well travelled American guests said it was as good as any hotel he had been in anywhere. Peggy loved to wake up early to watch the bridge beside the hotel open and the boats come in. Despite this apparent luxury, Peggy still found that ordinary people had very little and would want to come up and touch the visitors.

They were inevitably taken to Lenin's tomb which did not impress Peggy greatly. There was a scary moment as they were queuing to go in. One of the Americans took a photograph and had his camera confiscated by some rather fierce guards, but they politely and solemnly presented it back to him when he left!

Russia was just opening up to visitors and so they were taken to see factories at work, and to see the workers themselves with whom they had lunch. Peggy was fascinated by the metal holders for the glasses in which they were served the milk-less tea, which seemed to be the only drink on offer. She was presented with one by a workman at the end of the visit. She brought it home and still treasures it today as a kindly given memento of her visit, a rather grubby looking grey metal holder albeit with some complex filigree work. It was not until 50 years later when it was cleaned that she found it was solid silver, probably a pre-revolution piece!

Cars were relatively new to most Russians and they were just becoming widely available. The standard of driving was terrifying, but the streets were beautifully clean, as prisoners were used to clean them constantly. The people were friendly and welcoming, and the dancing in the shows she saw was fantastic. She felt very privileged to go to Russia at the time when few western tourists could do so.

John Letts also arranged a trip to Pompeii with a group of archaeologists from whom Peggy learned a great deal about digs and about the marvellous city itself.

She had expected to see very little but wondered at the fact that she could walk in the wheel ruts which had been made by chariots and were perfectly preserved in the volcanic lava. Peggy sat in a garden which was supposed to be haunted and, although she did not really believe all the tales she heard, she definitely felt a presence there.

Hong Kong became a regular destination for Peggy over many years. Initially she went to instruct teachers how to teach drama in very basic local schools where junior and senior pupils had to attend in shifts. It was difficult for them to study in such conditions, but there was a great desire to learn and develop. Soon Peggy was going annually to adjudicate their festival, and then to help prepare more adjudicators for what became a major event. Peggy was delighted to see the schools develop into smart establishments with excellent facilities and uniforms, a massive improvement on those very poor beginnings. What remained unchanged was the tremendous enthusiasm and warm welcome which Peggy always received in Hong Kong.

Peggy had always longed to go to mainland China but travel there was rarely permitted in those early days. She had tried to go before the war by trying to get a job acting out information for the illiterate population. There had been just one small detail she had overlooked in this endeavour; she did not speak Mandarin or any of the other Chinese languages and so did not get the job!

She finally managed to wangle a visit to China, as the then Governor of Hong Kong permitted her to travel as his niece!

She had to travel on a grossly overloaded plane. One plane had broken down and so the Chinese put two plane loads of people on one flight and they had to sit on each other's laps! They stayed in an old hotel which was very basic and had walls literally like cardboard. There were no washing facilities and the lavatory arrangements were rudimentary and not at all private!

Peggy saw men, woman and children digging new roads by hand and girls making lace in damp and squalid conditions without proper light. Peggy was horrified that people were living and working in such conditions and kicked up a big fuss. Others in the party tried to silence her, feeling an international incident about to erupt!

Such interesting experiences only served to give Peggy get more material to work with and her pupils benefitted from her ever widening knowledge of the world and her connection with people wherever she went.

Rock bottom

Peggy remained deeply devoted to her parents. Her beloved Father died in 1973, and she and her Mother lived in a house behind the School. Her Mother suffered a stroke and gradually became more incapacitated, but lived on until December 1978. During her Mother's final illness, Peggy found it difficult to cope with the business side of running the School. Her maths had not greatly improved over the years and it was an aspect of the School she did not enjoy. She had had a good and trustworthy staff and had been content to leave the business element to them. Unfortunately, coinciding with her Mother's decline, a new person was employed to deal with the finances. This proved disastrous and money was siphoned off. Ultimately the crime was discovered, but too late. The business was ruined and despite having a full roll, Peggy was compelled to lay off her faithful staff and sell up. She was pleased that the local press did not blame her for what had happened and was glad that she had built up such a good relationship with them over the years. She had had excellent friends within the whole community around the School and frequently had supported local charities with special shows. The Jewish community were particularly supporters of the school and many Jewish children had become pupils. She had a particularly good relationship with Rabbi Shebson, but did not always agree with him as an adjudicator, as he tended to want to reward children whose parents best supported the Synagogue! They argued over many a judgement when working together, but Peggy usually won the day!

Peggy had ended up with virtually nothing and had to rely on individual work and examining for income, although for some time she continued to teach Ridley pupils to get them through their various examinations.

CHAPTER 8

ARTHUR AGAIN

Peggy had not forgotten Arthur, nor he her.

He had had a highly successful and fulfilling career, retiring as an Air Commodore. He had been married with two daughters, but he was lonely after his wife died. He always carried Peggy's photo and sometimes showed it to close friends. He had tried to trace her through Equity but at a time when she was no longer performing. She also had thought of him and decided to try to trace him via the RAF, which was more successful. She received a memo back from her enquiry saying that Air Commodore Clegg was retired from the RAF and giving his address in Wendover in Buckinghamshire. She wrote a very neutral note to him, not sure if he would want any contact. But happily Arthur was delighted to hear from her and on 4th March 1984 he wrote,

"Now I know spring has arrived as your letter brought all of the flowers in my garden into bloom"

They agreed to meet and the years rolled back and their relationship rekindled. As Peggy told the local paper later,

"I knew I still felt the same way but I was worried about meeting him in case he did not live up to my memories. But we met at Easter and I needn't have worried. He is still the same darling man, a little balder and a little plumper, but I recognised him instantly"

Arthur, within days, had decided that he had walked away from Peggy twice, once in India and once in London, and he was not going to make the same mistake again. He wanted to get married, but Peggy was not sure how his daughters would feel about that. She trod carefully, meeting one and then the other and finally saying "yes" when they told her that their Father would be very happy with her. "Please marry Father," they implored.

Arthur resumed writing love letters to Peggy as he had during the war until they got married and he continued to do so if she worked away during their marriage, particularly when she made her annual visit to Hong Kong as festival adjudicator. They show that his love for her remained as strong as ever over the years, and there is a sense of incredulity that they managed to pick up the threads so well after so long.

Peggy and Arthur married on 1st September 1984 on the 40th anniversary of their meeting in 1944.

(Peggy and Arthur marry)

Peggy moved to Wendover and they had nearly ten very happy years together until Arthur's death on 7th March 1994. Peggy says that meeting up with Arthur again was a miracle and she treasured the time they had together, not that it was all plain sailing. Arthur was a lifelong smoker and Peggy abhorred smoking, but he gave up, although his temper was not good during the process. Arthur loved his meat, Peggy was a vegetarian. Arthur would not let her cook meat for him and so they found a solution, eating out at a local restaurant every Sunday which catered for both of them, Arthur enjoying his roast lunch and Peggy the vegetarian dishes.

They travelled, met each other's friends and made up for so many lost years. Jersey was a particular favourite destination, although Arthur was very upset when he lost his wedding ring swimming there. Peggy was also upset as she had given him her Father's ring as his wedding ring, but she could not let him see that she minded too much.

Peggy continued working both as an examiner, freelance teacher and voice coach at The Arts Educational School in Tring. Arthur was her rock and her support. He loved to be protective and helpful, insisting he drove her to many of her work commitments. Peggy, an excellent driver and well used to looking after herself after so many independent years, had to find tactful ways to take over the driving which was not Arthur's strength! She particularly loved driving her red American Ford Mustang, and retains a love of fast cars still.

It was a joy to her to come home to him after a day's teaching, and to find Arthur had the tea ready, and they sat and talked over the day. He shared the inevitable highs and lows of teaching with her and they always discussed everything together.

Peggy also enjoyed the formal events that she went to as Arthur's wife as, although he was retired, the invitations to grand occasions still came.

(Arthur still looking good in uniform!)

She had been a republican, but, in true Peggy style, she became a monarchist on meeting the Queen. Indeed, feeling that Her Majesty had not been well briefed on one occasion, Peggy broke all protocols and took it upon herself to inform Her Majesty about the people she was meeting.

Arthur was not in good health; the years of smoking had taken their toll on his heart.

Peggy always knew that if Arthur died before her, she would not get a pension, as he had retired before their marriage. He told her this before they married, not that it made a jot of difference to her decision to marry, but Arthur, as ever, was very honourable and wanted her to understand the situation. After Arthur's death, Peggy joined the campaign to effect a change to this injustice in the system. She continues to fight, not just for herself but for others in a similar situation.

Arthur died unexpectedly in his sleep in 1994. Although he was not in good health, Peggy had not thought the end was close. Arthur's death was a deep blow to Peggy, but it was slightly softened by the care and attention of her stepdaughters, and of course, her many friends. Peggy was in the middle of judging a festival in Peterborough over two weekends when Arthur died midweek. Her friends, Max and Nesta, were always her hosts for these weekend events. They were amazed that she returned for the second weekend, but however upset she was, Peggy always carried on with the show.

Indeed Peggy even managed to speak at Arthur's funeral and say publically a final goodnight to her "sweet Prince".

She had thoroughly enjoyed the unexpected ten happy years they had together, and many a lesser spirit may have rather given up on life at this point, but not so Peggy!

CHAPTER 9

LATER CAREER

As well as teaching, examining and adjudicating, Peggy continued performing and giving talks and recitals to many local groups. Her work was also widely recognised over the years in the profession and honours and letters after her name were heaped upon her—F.G.S.M., F.S.T.S.D., F.V.C.M. and F.R.S.A.—to name but some. One would like to think Miss Sprules would have approved and Miss Swan would no longer be bitterly disappointed!

Peggy also threw herself into researching her illustrious ancestor Bartholomew Gosnold, the explorer who founded Jamestown. She researched the family tree and found that down the generations there was always a Robert in the family—which was of course her little brother's name. She travelled to see the places where Gosnold had settled with her cousin, and is proud of her famous forebear. His adventures are worthy of a separate book, but perhaps his zest for adventure and willingness to try new experiences have been handed down the generations.

She also has found that another member of the family on the Spiller side invented the pince-nez and she loves to delve into her family's history. As with every family, she has found a few minor scandals. The Spiller great grandmother had Protestant children with her English husband and Catholic children with her French lover, and Peggy remembers visiting a great aunt who was a nun. This lady had had to flee to England from the German invasion of France during the Great War, and ended her days in great pain from arthritis, which she saw as a penance for past sins. She was somewhat shocked by her forthright great niece asking loudly what bloody sins could she have committed!!

Peggy has recorded books for the blind and disabled and even returned finally to work for the BBC in 2001, recording episodes of Dr Who with Stephen Fry for the radio and internet version, and with small parts in television dramas such as "Holby City", "My Hero" and "The Queen's Sister".

She finally decided that she would give up television work at the age of 92, when her legendary ability to learn lines finally failed her, and after many years of examining and adjudication in Hong Kong she decided to call it a day in 2008. Peggy no longer travels abroad, but still will work locally and still inspires her pupils and enthrals her audiences at WI, U3A and Church events, and, however, tired she may feel, as soon as she steps onto a stage, she becomes a radiant performer again.

Never a dull moment (conclusion)

Some long time ago, Peggy wrote on a scrap of paper that the story of her life should begin, "Unfinished business—the road not taken—the story of my life", which sounds rather negative. She also thought "If only . . . ." may have been a possible title for this book, as she feels there have been many moments when her impetuous nature has led her to make the wrong decision, usually without much consideration, and she feels she could have achieved much more in her professional life especially, if only . . . .

However, when she gives talks to various groups about her life, she entitles it, "Never a dull moment!" This is perhaps the more apt description of such a full, varied and busy existence, and the title we finally chose for the book. Life is certainly never dull with Peggy and the story of this extraordinary life enthrals her audiences. In her nineties, Peggy remains lively, vivacious, amusing and mildly flirtatious. She dresses impeccably, her voice remains strong, her love of people and genuine interest in them is undiminished. She will try new experiences, rarely refuses an invitation and volunteers for charity and community work with a zest seldom seen in people half her age.

Her scrap of paper suggests the end to her autobiography should be

"I am now 95 years old and there is still the final road to take . . . . unfinished business . . . ."

It has been a privilege to help to tell Peggy's story but one cannot help but feel that there are still many paths to be explored before the final road.

(Peggy's first Pimms aged 91)

Lightning Source UK Ltd.
Milton Keynes UK
UKOW052032090212

187014UK00002B/2/P